BUILDING AND MANAGING HIGH-PERFORMANCE DISTRIBUTED TEAMS

NAVIGATING THE FUTURE OF WORK

Alberto S. Silveira Jr.

Apress®

Building and Managing High-Performance Distributed Teams: Navigating the Future of Work

Alberto S. Silveira Jr.
Mount Kisco, NY, USA

ISBN-13 (pbk): 978-1-4842-7054-7   ISBN-13 (electronic): 978-1-4842-7055-4
https://doi.org/10.1007/978-1-4842-7055-4

Managing Director, Apress Media LLC: Welmoed Spahr
Acquisitions Editor: Susan McDermott
Development Editor: Rita Fernando
Coordinating Editor: Rita Fernando

Cover designed by eStudioCalamar

Distributed to the book trade worldwide by Springer Science+Business Media New York, 1 New York Plaza, New York, NY 100043. Phone 1-800-SPRINGER, fax (201) 348-4505, e-mail orders-ny@springer-sbm.com, or visit www.springeronline.com. Apress Media, LLC is a California LLC and the sole member (owner) is Springer Science + Business Media Finance Inc (SSBM Finance Inc). SSBM Finance Inc is a **Delaware** corporation.

For information on translations, please e-mail booktranslations@springernature.com; for reprint, paperback, or audio rights, please e-mail bookpermissions@springernature.com.

Apress titles may be purchased in bulk for academic, corporate, or promotional use. eBook versions and licenses are also available for most titles. For more information, reference our Print and eBook Bulk Sales web page at http://www.apress.com/bulk-sales.

Any source code or other supplementary material referenced by the author in this book is available to readers on GitHub via the book's product page, located at www.apress.com/9781484270547. For more detailed information, please visit http://www.apress.com/source-code.

Printed on acid-free paper

To my wife Caroline, my daughter Sophia, and my parents Alberto and Inez.

Contents

About the Author

Alberto S. Silveira Jr. is a passionate, energetic, and hands-on executive with many years of experience in building teams. He believes strongly that people always come first and uses trust as the foundation of his success. He loves the art of gathering people as much as he likes being out on the water in his boat. Since his earliest years growing up in Brazil, Alberto has proven himself as a natural leader who leverages his ability to learn quickly and adapt to change, which has allowed him to provide technical and product vision that accelerates value within the organizations that he has worked for or consulted to. At the heart of all of his corporate activities is a blend of leadership, empathy, and creative and analytical abilities that he uses to guide his teams toward maximum effectiveness.

Acknowledgments

Many friends and colleagues have been instrumental in developing the ideas in this book, including (in no particular order) Luciano Oliveira, Brian Blount, Guilherme Althoff, Sam Marx, John Patton, Rodrigo Cunha, Alex Martins, Marcelo Camacho, and Joel Hames. I'm also profoundly grateful to Steve Prentice for the support and the uncountable hours spent helping make this book come true.

The creation of this book would not have been possible without the expertise and partnership of Ubiminds (https://ubiminds.com). They have been paving a path toward the future of work for many years helping their customers build successful high-performance teams. Thanks for all the feedback, sponsorship, and belief in the importance of building people-first organizations.

Lastly, I would like to thank my family starting with my wife, Caroline, for being the most loving partner I could wish for. I also want to thank my daughter, Sophia, for her pure and genuine love. Finally, I would like to thank my parents, Alberto and Inez, for raising me in the simplest way possible, teaching me how to live in this world to always do what's right.

Foreword: Following My Own Personal True North

It was a blistering summer morning when I stepped outside and smelled a tantalizing aroma that could only mean one thing—someone was getting ready for a cookout. Following my nose, and inspired by my love for summer gatherings, I wandered across the street to identify the source of that incredible aroma. I first noticed a large rack of ribs being slowly cooked over an open flame in a manner I'd never seen before. And shortly thereafter, I noticed an affable and jovial man, whom I had never met previously, standing near the fire tending to this enticing cut of meat. Within a matter of seconds, I found myself being invited to come back in a few hours to enjoy the feast and was encouraged to bring my entire family.

When we arrived later that afternoon, I was impressed by the sheer volume of people gathered, and I was drawn in by the relaxing sounds of island music—it was as if I was instantly transported to an island party somewhere in the Caribbean, but in reality, I was in suburban New York.

While my neighbor seemed occupied by making his rounds with various guests, I did the socially appropriate thing and began to engage in conversation with the various folks who had gathered. I was instantly struck by the consistency in which folks described their **LOVE** for my neighbor, Alberto. Person after person described him as loyal, genuine, transparent, caring, fun-loving, and reliable. And even more surprising was to learn how these people first met Alberto and that most of them are either current or former employees with whom he has worked.

Consistently, one by one, I would hear stories of how they have followed Alberto from company to company, and when Alberto had success, so did they. This was the start of a journey that has led to one of the most rewarding personal relationships of my life. The years that have followed this event have involved many more cookouts and many new friendships with the folks I encountered on that warm summer day. We have since had the joy of raising our families together, listening to thousands of hours of music together, and enjoying numerous priceless afternoons on the lake with Alberto, sharing our love of life, family, friends, and helping others.

Very quickly, we learned that our professional passions aligned as well as our personal values. You see, I am a Licensed Clinical Psychologist and Organizational Development Specialist who has spent over a decade helping individuals and organizations achieve their desired change. In addition to maintaining a small private practice and consulting on the side, I work full-time as the Chief Quality Officer at a federally run hospital that is part of the largest integrated healthcare system in the United States.

In my evolving discussions with Alberto about our professional approaches and experiences, I have learned of his passion for building teams and advancing organizations, which directly aligns with what drives me professionally. Where we differed was that Alberto had a knack for working in agile startup environments and helping young companies mature in the right way, avoiding the pitfalls of profit-driven traditional companies where bureaucracy and bottom-line focus supersede mission and people-driven organizations.

On one of our more recent boating excursions, I learned of his desire to write a book that would share his approaches to building remote teams while maintaining the essential commitment to the organizational ethos necessary to become successful. And as many of us do, I found myself applying the principles and practices he so passionately spoke of to my personal experience working in a slow-moving, hierarchical, government agency. I found myself skeptical of these practices actually applying to my work setting, let alone other legacy-type companies.

Well, the COVID pandemic gave me an opportunity to test these theories. While running a healthcare system, obviously, requires the need to maintain a large on-premises presence, many of our administrative functions were challenged to adapt to a virtual setting to minimize traffic and potential exposure to COVID. As a supervisor for a team of 30-plus professionals, I needed to rapidly transition my department to a distributed team-based approach, and I knew exactly whom to call. In consultation with Alberto, I successfully navigated this seamless transition with an established, well-entrenched senior team and within the broader context of a large change-resistant organization.

It became evident that what Alberto spoke of represented a truism that applied to all types and sizes of companies. Whether you are seeking guidance on following your own personal true north as a leader or looking for how to better navigate this evolving world of virtually distributed employment, this book represents an easy read, grounded in firm evidence-based practices, delivered in an approachable manner by someone who lives and breathes what he writes about. I truly say that never in my life have my personal and professional philosophies better aligned and can simply be characterized by Alberto's motto of *"One Team, One Heart"*!

Dr. Michael Stern
Licensed Clinical Psychologist
Organizational Development Specialist
Prosci Change Management Professional
Lean Six Sigma Black Belt

Introduction

Whom Is This Book Written For?

I have written this book primarily for team leaders or officers of smallish companies, with populations in the tens through to the mid-hundreds. I have also written it for managers of somewhat autonomous departments within larger companies and for everyone who works with these leaders, because everyone in a company ultimately needs to know what being in a distributed team is all about. Empowerment comes from within as much as from above. Smaller companies have the greatest chance to remain agile and responsive, but departments within larger companies might also be empowered to move independently.

In general, I feel that companies with thousands of employees have already grown too big and are inevitably dominated by an internal infrastructure and bureaucracy that makes agility very difficult. From a nautical standpoint, it's like comparing a sailboat to a supertanker; you can't turn a supertanker on a dime. Departments such as human resources and finance often have their own agenda and politics. That doesn't mean that a department within a large organization is excluded from the ideas shared here, but there may be additional hurdles that will have to be considered for change to take effect.

Younger organizations tend to still be fueled by the energy of their startup years as well as the vision of their founders. They tend to still have the flexibility and fearlessness that allow them to examine new ideas and implement them more efficiently. But this is not an exclusive club. I feel that many companies that are older and have already weathered more than a few storms over their lifetime will benefit enormously from this coming change and are still qualified to be a part of it.

How Is This Book Organized?

This book has three main parts that all contribute to its main mission of building and managing high-performance distributed teams, by intertwining sailing analogies and business stories. Each chapter offers a three-bullet summary of its key message, and within each chapter I regularly refer back or forward to other chapters to highlight where a specific concept is spoken about in more detail. I do this because I do not expect everybody to read this book from cover to cover. That, too, is an assumption from a bygone era. Read what you need, and learn in your own time and in your own way.

Part 1: The Passion for the Voyage

Here I share some key concepts that I have discovered, developed, or refined during my career, which also speak to my passions about teams, and how to envision a cohesive and functional crew. Concepts include the North Star, the Iron Triangle, *One Team, One Heart*, and the various types of teams that can exist.

Part 2: Setting Sail

Next, I discuss some of the practical elements of getting started and getting out there. This includes building a distributed team, the need to use measurement and metrics, streamlining processes, fostering a culture of collaboration and continuous improvement, and hiring and retention strategies for onboarding the crew.

Part 3: Staying Shipshape

Although leadership by itself can be an overused word, the art of leading or commanding a vessel requires specific and careful leadership skills, which must be shown in words and actions. In this section, I discuss measuring mood and morale, the importance of the correct choice of words, developing the correct mindset, and sharing these with your distributed team through optimum leadership behavior.

Crossing the Equator

I had in my mind as I wrote this book the metaphor of crossing the Equator (www.crossingtheequator.com/). As an imaginary line that divides the planet, the Equator is hugely symbolic for several reasons that kept popping into my imagination and my memory. As a boater and competitive sailor, it plays a major role in maritime navigation and tradition, and to this day sailors and cruise ship passengers alike celebrate their first crossing of this dotted line. My passion for boating appears many times in this book because of the obvious parallels between crews on a boat and teams in an organization where navigation remains a vital tool for both.

Second is how the Equator mirrors my own life story, growing up in Brazil and having literally crossed the Equator to set foot in New York City, where I was able to pursue that American dream of building a successful career. My heart still beats for my home country, of course, and as my book clearly shows, we are in an age where it is more possible than ever to make a success of oneself from wherever in the world you happen to be. For me, the crossing of the Equator represents my commitment to go out there and take that leap, from raw talent and desire to tangible achievement.

Third, we are all crossing an equator right now for another lap around the globe. It is a cycle, and the world is shifting this time to one where people can leverage technology—the Internet especially—to work how they want from wherever they happen to be. Collaboration technologies are taking the place of brick-and-mortar meeting spaces, and this is leading to a tipping of the scales in terms of how work and life unfold for us all. The pandemic of 2020 pushed much of this activity into high gear, but even before that, the future-of-work gurus were pointing to a global economy with greater work opportunities for all, crossing over into an entirely new work model: "the new normal."

To succeed in any venture, you must chart your course and measure your progress in a way that you and your team can understand. The Equator is printed on every map and chart of our planet, and as such stands as a universally recognized symbol of transition.

The Passion for the Voyage

The Voyage

For centuries there has been a maritime tradition that when sailors cross the Equator for the first time, they undergo an initiation ceremony. The nature of the ceremony varies from country to country, but suffice to say, the crossing of this vital line of navigation is a meaningful symbol of progress for each crew member. It forms part of the ritual of team bonding for a crew that works hard, as a unit, on a ship. It is something that is overseen by any captain that understands the power of a tightly knit crew, and it signifies a literal crossover into new waters.

No matter what hemisphere a sailor considers to be home, the other hemisphere is decidedly different: the stars in the night sky are different, as are the currents, winds, and weather patterns. Hurricanes and other storms rotate in an opposite direction, and there's a new magnetic pole to locate. The Equator is a true dividing line for our rotating planet. It is not just an arbitrary mark on the map.

When people look back at the year 2020 and the pandemic that gripped the planet, they might discern a similar equatorial dividing line cutting directly across the working world. That was the year that everyone was essentially forced to become part of a work-related diaspora. We all had to take refuge in our homes and try to get things done from there. In one hemisphere, we had the "traditional way" of working, consisting of commutes, offices, and a large amount of physical togetherness. In the other hemisphere, we see work being done far away from a centralized office, with everything held together virtually by computers and Internet technology. In 2020, we were forced to cross the equator from one hemisphere to the other, faster than most of us would have imagined.

© Alberto S. Silveira Jr. 2021
A. S. Silveira Jr., *Building and Managing High-Performance Distributed Teams*,
https://doi.org/10.1007/978-1-4842-7055-4_1

Prior to 2020, there had been much discussion centered around concepts like remote work, working from home, and the gig economy—all of which seemed to be viable yet somewhat distant concepts. Many large organizations had started testing these ideas out minimally, usually to acknowledge the creeping awareness that younger employees especially would want to be more mobile than their elders, but also to see what the new interactive and collaborative technologies might be capable of. Yet there remained the conviction that real work was to be firmly anchored in the physical office.

As the pandemic spread across the world in the spring of 2020, companies, governments, and organizations were forced to retool extremely quickly. Their tentative plans for a slow shift to a more distributed workforce under the trendy mantle of *digital transformation* were pushed into overdrive. There was now no time to train employees and managers. They had to be sent home to set up shop there, right away.

Many of those whose jobs involved working primarily with a computer and email were in the fortunate position to at least have a laptop and an Internet connection in their homes, meaning that this revised version of their jobs was at least possible. The pandemic forced people and the companies that employed them to cross that equator and move into the era of the distributed team. We had been approaching it for years, but now it was here, and we had no choice but to sail over it onto the other side.

It is my belief that this other side, this era in which people work from somewhere other than a central office, is not a temporary thing. It represents a new frontier, the official start of a new era of work. It was going to happen anyway, but lockdown rushed it along like a strong tailwind. We have the technology available to us now that frees us from the need to travel a specific and single location.

But it's not just about technology. The distributed teams model also represents a new approach to time, organization, and relationships. It involves a novel intermingling of work lives and home lives. It requires a willingness among companies and employees to expand their definition of employment, given that people are no longer hemmed in by a fixed commuting distance. It demands a redefinition of leadership and trust, and it will force companies to reexamine what teams are, how they will work, and what types of physical spaces are needed and which are no longer needed for the years ahead.

The distributed teams model is an industrial revolution in its own right, and much like the revolutions that gave us steam power, electrical power, mass manufacturing, logistics, and computers, this one turns everything on its head once again, providing great opportunities for those who wish to embrace it.

Teams that operate outside a company's walls are different from traditional in-office arrangements, and they need to be understood for what they are and how they differ from each other. For decades, managers have sought to understand how best to manage and motivate their in-house employees, and they will now have to learn a new set of skills. We've crossed the equator. There's no going back to the way things were before.

We've crossed the equator. There's no going back to the way things were before.

This book is about how to build, manage, and understand high-performance distributed teams, which I feel will be the core of business processes in this new era. Many teams around the globe had already been operating in this central and vital way prior to the 2020 pandemic, but in smaller numbers. What was already a well-established work in progress was pushed into high gear during lockdown, forcing businesses across all industries to adapt quickly.

In this book, I will describe what distributed teams are and what they are not, how they work, how they compare to other types of external teams, what they need, what you'll need as a team manager, and how to maximize a team's performance. I believe my past and current work experience, paired with my own passions, make me qualified to at least share my experiences, definitions, and visions around this new management technique.

I hope also that my observations will help you make an informed decision, whether you are a team leader, a team member, an entrepreneur, or a C-level executive. Although my stories come from the software industry, I think you will find these approaches apply to all types of business environments, regardless of what products or services you deliver and regardless of your size and reach.

In today's business world, change happens in minutes, not months. This takes many people by surprise, especially those in positions of management and decision-making, because even when they are aware of this accelerated pace of change, it often proves difficult to pivot quickly. So, in this book, I will lay out the concepts behind the high-performance distributed teams model as best I can. I will use up-to-date facts and case studies, and I will also share stories from my other life, out on the water.

Heading Out from the Harbor

When I am not at my desk, I am a boater. There is nothing I love more than steering my powerboat out past the safe and secure walls of a breakwater, past the lighthouse, and toward the open sea. That moment of transition from harbor to ocean is breathtaking. It's more than a line on a map. To me it represents another boundary, just like the Equator, a dividing line between two worlds.

I also crew on racing sailboats, often in regattas in the Mediterranean. Being out on water is what I live for. To me, it represents a point of intersection where nature meets the refined technology and engineering of modern watercraft, as well as the mental, physical, and social capacities of their human crews.

Back on land, I am an expert in software products and the teams that build them. The passion that fuels my boating life spills over into my professional work, and I have found so many parallels that I thought it would be great to share some of them as a way of explaining the distributed teams concept and of bringing it to life. It makes learning much more fun and helps to keep facts memorable.

For a start, boating is not a one-person endeavor. Not even for those fearless people who decide to do a solo voyage across the Atlantic or the Pacific or around Africa. Even they need a team behind them, for strategizing, logistics, and maybe even rescue. Boating demands teamwork. You can never be truly alone—in fact, you *must* never be truly alone. Every boater must rely on others, not only the people who make up your crew but other boaters too, who must all understand and respect the rules of the water. This has been a truth and a tradition for centuries.

At the same time, a boat is a community unto itself. Out there on the ocean, it is a self-contained unit in which people must work and live together. People have been taking to the water by boat for thousands of years, meaning there are many techniques that have been perfected over this time, specifically for the closely and clearly defined quarters of a vessel. These, I feel, can be transferred, either directly or through extrapolation, to the team-based work environments of today and, more importantly, of tomorrow. These include management of crews, communication, and overall efficient organizational procedures.

Furthermore, a boat is a marvelous symbol of business, given that it is an evolving technology that has been used over the centuries for all forms of human endeavor, including exploration, sustenance, commerce, and war. Everywhere you look throughout history, boats have had an impact in some way.

The art and science of managing distributed teams in an ever-evolving business climate has much in common with that of boating. You must never lose sight of your people or of your bearings. How your team—or your crew—performs will depend on each person's level of knowledge and experience, their commitment and mood, their ability to communicate and understand, their level of self-empowerment, and the structure of rules and guidelines that will make it all work together, regardless of the type of weather they face.

So I will share some boating stories and use some nautical metaphors to explain my concepts, because I am already well known for them as a manager and as a leader, and frankly, I think they match up well. I have developed these stories over the years partly because English is my second language, which means I like to paint a picture with metaphors to make up for those words or phrases that might still be missing from my English language vocabulary. But also, metaphors have long been used by educators and leaders because they connect with our inner child—the one that always loves to hear a story. Stories connect with people better than straight-up facts do.

In a world dominated by computer screens, meeting rooms, and, more recently, social distancing and video chats, I feel I can best express the genuine love and passion I have for helping companies pull themselves successfully into the future by channeling the elation I feel every time my crew and I head out on another adventure and that salt spray stings my face once again.

What Is a Distributed Team and Why Is It So Important Right Now?

At the heart of a distributed team is a group of people who are able to work together as part of a company, team, or project, from wherever they happen to be, as opposed to being physically located in a central office. In fact, as I will describe in more detail throughout this book, a distributed team is one in which *all* the members are somewhere other than the central office, so that there is no center. That is what differentiates a *distributed team* from just having some people working remotely. There's a big difference between these two concepts, and just knowing that, and its impact on your business going forward, will be of major strategic value.

Distributed teams are held together not just by technology, but also through a renewed approach to leadership, communication, culture, and project management. The way in which they are managed has a great deal of sway on how well they will perform, but again, it's not just about the technology. A racing sailboat doesn't win competitions just because it is a well-built watercraft. Victory depends just as much, if not more, on the crew, how well its members work together, how they communicate, and how they are looked after and guided by the captain.

This is all so very important right now because distributed teams are quickly becoming a central pillar of the future of work. Those who declared the whole video chat thing to be a tedious failure, for example, were often the people who had not yet had the chance to learn that distributed work is not the same as on-premises work. You cannot simply *lift and shift* or copy and paste the habits of the office and expect them to work out there in the field. There is a huge difference between being "at home trying to work" and "working from home."

The *lift and shift* response is typical of every technological revolution. When the motion picture was invented over a century ago, the first movies were simply stage plays captured on film. It was the same for television. It took decades for these media to come into their own, and they're still evolving today. Early websites were formatted like books, and early music videos really did not know what to do with themselves.

Sophistication and maturity come from continuous usage and improvement, and we are in the earliest of days of a new era of distributed collaboration. The assumption that just because everyone has the technology, they all know how to use it, is erroneous yet predictable. For example, a video chat meeting is not just about turning the camera on. This is a medium that needs its users to know how to convey trust and respect, encourage independence, support flexibility and openness toward homelife schedules, and maintain morale, all the while ensuring that productivity and quality remain high.

The point is business and commerce are changing fast, and so are the jobs that make business happen. So, too, are the types of people who work these jobs, and as a result, those who wish to manage them and build success within their organizations must change too.

Why You Need to Read This Book

Most people that I have met at the various companies I have worked with share a few things in common. No matter what level their job is at, they are proud of doing good work. As individuals, they appreciate opportunities to advance, and they also like to feel they are part of a community. People want to make some sort of impact. They want to make a difference because, in the end, they care about and believe in what they do. That is the best anyone— any leader—can ask for. When people are there for a purpose, with their minds and soul, high performance finds a place to grow.

During the era of the First Industrial Revolution, companies needed hundreds of people to occupy the same physical space to turn raw material into finished products under a single roof. Whether it was textiles, steel, automobiles, or tomorrow's newspaper, the only way to get the job done was to have everyone onsite, because that's where the machinery, materials, and people were.

In those days, meetings could only be done through the power of speaking loudly in a room full of people. Boardrooms, classrooms, and churches, it was all the same. You had to show up in order to learn. Teleconferences and video chats were dreams of the future. From the days of the First Industrial Revolution up to the early 1960s, meetings could only be effectively done when everyone was together in a room. Teleconferences only became economically viable in the mid-1960s, and similarly, video conferences, which had been first demonstrated at the 1964 World's Fair, had to wait 30 more years. For project managers planning out tasks and timelines, the technologies were strictly analog: slide rules for calculation and plans written on sheets of paper stuck to the wall. Nevertheless, this humble approach helped fight the Second World War, it got the space program going, and set the stage for the computer revolution.

But now we live in the age of connectivity, where smart technologies allow production, innovation, and collaboration to all be far more agile and widespread. The shift from a centralized workplace model to a decentralized, distributed one forms part of the Fourth Industrial Revolution, a concept coined by Klaus Schwab, Executive Chairman of the World Economic Forum, in 2016. The concept of the distributed team is as vital to this current technological revolution as steam power was to the First Industrial Revolution two centuries earlier.

INDUSTRIAL REVOLUTIONS

Just in case you're interested, here's a summary of the four industrial revolutions:

- The first (1760–1840) used water and steam power to mechanize production.

- The second (1871–1914) used electric power to create mass production.

- The third (1960–2000) used electronics and information technology to automate production.

- The fourth (present day) builds on the third and is characterized by a fusion of technologies that blurs lines between the physical, digital, and biological spheres.[1]

Schwab points out that the reason why this Fourth Industrial Revolution stands on its own rather than being an offshoot of the third is because it's not about the tools and technology *per se*, but what is happening because of them, specifically, "velocity, scope, and systems impact," especially with regard to experiencing change and innovation at an exponential rate.[2]

---

[1]Paraphrased from "The Fourth Industrial Revolution: What it means, how to respond," by Klaus Schwab, retrieved from www.weforum.org/agenda/2016/01/the-fourth-industrial-revolution-what-it-means-and-how-to-respond/
[2]Ibid.

Where at one time a workforce was constrained by distance—companies generally hired people who lived close enough to be able to commute to the workplace daily—we now have the options as workers, managers, and customers to interact with people all over the world. Internet-enabled communication has been available to the public since 1990, but only in the past couple of years has its capacity been great enough to offer up features like live video and swift transfer of large files.

As more people gravitate to it as a new and better way to work, the managers and leaders who recognize the potential of this change will be the ones who will contribute the most to their company's future successes. We have barely just crossed the equator, meaning most people are still looking at this new hemisphere with old eyes. They continue to view video chats as a poor replacement for in-person meetings. They cannot grasp that a person can work better from a connected home office than from a cubicle. They do not understand how skills such as trust, empathy, and empowerment can replace command-and-control from a closed-door office.

We have barely crossed the equator. Most people are still looking at this new hemisphere with old eyes.

The future of work, as the experts like to call it, is inextricably tied to communication and collaboration—between technology and between people. My experiences, in working with business technology and the companies that use it, might be of help to you in creating what we boaters call a "float plan," that vital document that describes how you will take on your next adventure out on the open water.

Key Takeaways

- We are crossing into a new era in which distributed teams have become, and will remain, a reality for organizations of all sizes.

- The distributed teams construct cannot be simply a lift and shift of the traditional onsite activities.

- It's not just about technology; it's about teams and people and comprises part of the Fourth Industrial Revolution.

My Own Voyage Across the Equator

I have spent most of my life thus far as an engineer, specifically a software engineer. I love the profession and its traditions. I even love the word *engineer*. It has the air of someone who knows—or wants to know—where all the parts go and who has an affinity for the way they move and come alive, whether those parts are mechanical or digital—cogs or code. Everything is an engine of some sort.

I grew up in the city of Florianópolis, one of four cities referred to collectively as the Silicon Valley of Brazil. Florianópolis is close to the southernmost point of Brazil, south of Rio de Janeiro and about halfway down the South American continent. After earning a degree in computer science from a university there, I crossed the Equator and came to the United States in 2006 at the age of 25. I earned an MBA in New York and have been leading and managing teams, building software products, ever since.

My software engineering career actually started back in Brazil, during my childhood. I grew up in a family of five, and my father was the sole breadwinner.

© Alberto S. Silveira Jr. 2021
A. S. Silveira Jr., *Building and Managing High-Performance Distributed Teams*,
https://doi.org/10.1007/978-1-4842-7055-4_2

His monthly paycheck seldom saw us through the entire month, so like most people in the world, we had to make do. Although my father came from a very humble background himself, he was able to craft and maintain a career as an electronics specialist. In fact, he was a pioneer in the field of caller ID technology in Brazil.

The technology was called BINA, which is a Portuguese colloquialism meaning "person B identifies person A." He was developing and perfecting this back in the late 1980s, before cellphones and smartphones were the ubiquitous do-everything tool they are today. I am proud of what my father achieved, as, I believe, was he. He helped transform telecom centers to allow caller ID technology to work in Brazil. That helped Brazilian citizens embark on a path of technological innovation, and it's also what put food on our table.

Electronics tend to break after a while, which was good for me. It meant that on one side of our house there was a treasure trove of discarded circuit boards, transistors, and other components of a growing digital industry. I was fascinated with them, and I soon learned how to solder. I became quite good at troubleshooting broken or defective circuit boards, disassembling two or more of them in order to rebuild a complete, functional one that we were then able to sell. From microchips and transistors, I studied and tinkered with everything I could find, and this started me on my path to programming.

These days, most of us would have a hard time living without caller ID. We take it totally for granted. So it feels good to be able to say, "I was there at the beginning." I remember when the first landline caller IDs had the *amazing* capability of storing ten or more recently called numbers. That was a lot back then, yet even then we heard that classic argument from people who asked, "Why would we need that?" or "Why would we ever need more than that?"

This was something I would hear many times as I moved forward in the world of software development. Most people tend to approach change by looking back at what they have or what they fear they might lose, rather than forward to what they might gain. "Why do you need GPS in your car?" they asked in the mid-1990s. "Why would you want a camera in a phone?" they asked in the early 2000s. "How can I trust a tap-enabled debit card?" they asked in the 2010s. This constant pushback against change was one of those truths that made me realize that introducing people to innovative and progressive work habits would be equally difficult.

It was inevitable that the swift evolution of communication technology, along with the attitudes I observed in people both for and against it, would interact with my innate love for engineering and that altogether these items would guide me along my career path. I enjoyed seeing how, from a physical perspective, when things go together—when they fit together and move together—better things happen.

These experiences, first in Brazil and even now when I live in the United States, helped me crystallize in my mind the three different and fundamental building blocks to performance: the drive, the tools, and the people. You cannot understand or work with any of these if you don't understand all of them.

Wherever I worked, my goal was to eventually become the organization's head of engineering, so I could gain the authority needed to implement the ideas and processes that had become part of my professional experience and education. My ethos back then was the same as it is now, and that it will always be: "I must believe in the company's mission, and I'm always committed to giving the best of myself." This is just a fundamental rule that I follow whether I am out on the water, in the boardroom, or leading a team on a video chat. I apply the same principles that I've learned early in life: *If you are willing to do something, do it right.*

If you are willing to do something, do it right.

Connecting the Dots and the Stars

The challenge in many organizations happens when people try to connect the dots and get waylaid by biases or inadequate information or, worse, when they find they are too busy to even remember to make such connections. The dots I describe here are metaphorical of course, and they refer to critical thinking skills and strategic processes. They are vital to the successful navigation of a team and its priorities, but remain sadly underused.

Connecting dots has a direct historical connection to our ancestors and the stars. For centuries, humans have made sense of the bewildering blanket of stars in the night sky by drawing imaginary lines and creating constellations. This helped give meaning to the mysteries of the world in the prescientific age. Navigating the seas by starlight was a vital skill, made easier by identifying the constellations.

In business, those dots may be points within the process, metrics, steps toward a future goal, or any combination of these. The act of connecting them is an act of documenting them and of understanding their relationships, which is vital to understanding where you are and where you want to be. As a result, the central point of these connections, on paper as it is in the northern sky, is called the North Star.

I will talk in more depth about the North Star in Chapter 4, but suffice to say at this moment that a company might be able to identify its North Star as the unchanging definition of its purpose, but may still lack the communication or execution skills to move toward it. Or maybe it lost sight of it long ago, or perhaps it never defined it at all. When these things happen, a company's voyage becomes unsuccessful due to too much or too little process or an excess of bureaucracy and politics. These then obscure the sightlines between a company's vision, the internal user experience (UX), and ultimately the customer experience, creating further confusion and disappointment.

When people in positions of leadership misalign their teams and their North Star, their organizations struggle and sometimes fail. I have worked with many different leaders in my career. Some were really good, both as leaders and as mentors. Others? Well, let me put it this way: I don't miss them. However, from both of these groups, I have learned great lessons in terms of what to do and what not to do. There's always a life lesson in every experience, good or bad.

All of this led me to the decision to steer my career toward management and leadership positions, so that I could implement what I firmly believed to be the right thing to do. To me, this meant giving people access to their North Star once again and creating guidelines and a culture of trust to help them stay on the correct course.

One Team, One Heart

Managers tend to manage based on what they themselves have learned, some of it on the job and some of it in school, but a large and influential part of their approach to work comes from what they observed growing up. It's inevitable that all of us will register and remember much of what we experienced in our formative years. The impressions we make about the world at this time will never leave us, and they cannot help but influence the decisions we make about everything. This is one of the main reasons why the work from home style of a distributed team is hard to accept for managers who, in their childhood, watched one or both parents leave for work every day and who themselves had to travel to a classroom in a school somewhere to get an education.

When I was ten years old, there was no Internet, no social media, and no cellphones. I hadn't yet made up my mind as to what my career was going to be—I mean very few ten-year-old kids can do this—but there were hints about my future all around me. In addition to the wonderful pile of scrapped computer parts that I tinkered with, I also loved organizing soccer leagues within the neighborhood. I remember seeking out investments from local businesses to sponsor the league, buy jerseys, and so on.

So even though I work today with technologies that hadn't existed during my youth, I notice now how my attractions to technology and to team dynamics were evolving side by side. My experiences with my local soccer leagues helped me learn how to set goals, collaborate with people, and understand the need for processes and guidelines. I loved seeing the teams together, and

I really enjoyed watching the team members themselves share their enthusiasm for being part of an organized league. That's how I eventually came up with the term *One Team, One Heart*.

One Team, One Heart is the synergy that comes from people feeling good about their place in a highly productive team. It becomes a focal point, the heart of the team.

I practice *One Team, One Heart* everywhere I can, in meetings and on projects. We are one team, regardless how geographically far apart we are, no matter the person's religion, skin color, nationality, gender orientation, or physical ability. If a person is a good fit, then the moment we connect as simply humans becomes the foundation of a high-performance team. This ability to connect as humans, to socially and emotionally fuel people's individual desires to excel in their efforts—this is what I consider to be the true North Star of any business.

Driven Home Through Lockdown

In mentioning the COVID-19 pandemic, it is essential to first pause and think about the hundreds of thousands of people who perished, those who loved them, and the first responders and medical personnel who cared for them and who were also affected.

At the company I was working at, we were lucky, from a preparedness standpoint. We had been using a distributed teams approach for years prior to 2020, and so when lockdown came, our teams were familiar with it from a work and cultural point of view. While other companies were questioning how or even if they could train their employees and management into this new approach, my teams were already working at high efficiency. I say this not to gloat at a time of global tragedy, but at least to acknowledge that an approach that had been designed for a planned transition called *digital transformation* also worked well during the period of forced transition known as *pandemic lockdown*.

As a global culture, we were literally driven home, to self-isolate and seek to avoid the contagion. At the same time, the idea of the distributed teams model was being figuratively driven home in the minds of employees and managers everywhere.

It's easy to see how this *distributed teams* concept could fail miserably for an office-centric company in such a moment of crisis. A manager who is used to walking the halls and calling meetings will have a hard time coming to grips with an empty building and a home-based workforce. Many leaders feel safer when they can see their people physically there in the office. Face time becomes the primary factor in helping them believe their people are working diligently. Although this concept has been ruthlessly mocked in TV shows and movies, it remains the *de facto* definition of work.

Trust became the key differentiator between managers who were able to embrace a work from home model during lockdown and those who couldn't. *Trust.* You either feel it or you don't. For every proactive manager who embraced collaboration technology and trusted their team members to work from off-site locations, there were many others who fundamentally distrusted all of it and expressed that distrust openly.

Consequently, for many managers and leaders, the result was—and still is—chaos. They have no idea what to do in terms of building a distributed team. They might be able to shape an initial concept, but they have no true map and definitely no guarantee of stability upon which to build a solid plan, and this jeopardizes everything—the company, the team, and their own career.

How Unicorns Lose Their Magic

The ability to handle change is a hallmark of the aging process in companies. Startups, in their early stages, have a lot to think about. They are often still immersed in the heady mindset of the aggressive innovator, seeking to change the world with a new idea and an angel investor at their side. They are in unicorn mode. Tesla and Amazon used to be like that. So did Facebook once upon a time, and before them Google and before them Microsoft.

These were all startups, often created or enhanced by a single individual or a small group, who were energetic, brilliant, and fearless. They had a new product, and they wanted to bring it to market in a way that would change the world. In the era before Microsoft, large, long-in-the-tooth companies like IBM and Hewlett Packard dominated the landscape. These companies, too, had visionaries at the helm at one time, as did Chrysler, Ford, and Boeing. But the building of a company was different back then: more structured, formal, and devoted to a more traditional management culture and hierarchy—inherited from industrial models of work.

The information age needed to occur in order for ground-breaking products like Napster to change the music industry, paving the way for Spotify and iTunes, and Netflix, paving the way for the proliferation of digital media streaming services. The list of aggressive successful innovators gets more crowded the further along the timeline you go, to the point, today, where every individual with an Internet connection has the wisdom of the entire planet literally at their fingertips and can become world famous overnight with a single online video or a single good idea.

But it is inevitable that these aggressive new-era innovators, as they age, follow the same physical trajectories as all human beings do. They mature, they grow a little fatter around the middle, and their adventurous spirit is replaced by caution and nostalgia. This starts when the unicorn amasses so much wealth so quickly that it must install a parent figure in the CEO position, to ensure there are experienced adults in the room, ostensibly to manage growth at scale. Then post-IPO, or post-acquisition, the company finds itself under the guidance of a board of directors, accountants, and lawyers.

What was once three people living off pizza and coffee and sleeping on the office sofa becomes an organization that has growing departments and whose motivations are driven more by shareholder expectations than a burning ideology. New leaders are headhunted in, new processes are introduced, but they transform into a type of ergonomic inflation, following a law of diminishing returns in which additional resources fail to generate corresponding progress. It's like turning the boat upside down and expecting it to go faster.

I feel that traditional human resources (HR) is something of an outdated concept, as is traditional IT and finance. I will talk more about how the choices of words matter in Chapter 12, but referring to humans as *resources* is not right to me. Enterprise organizations often have no idea how much traditional organizational silos cost and how processes and bureaucracy actually impact their ability to maneuver and quickly adapt to fast-changing market conditions, causing further misalignment with the original North Star. These departments often have their own agendas and possibly even their own particular North Star, which is seldom about the customer, the user, or the product. From a nautical perspective, I often think that those departments are so far from the boat, they are actually inland and not even facing the sea.

Going Distributed Is Not What You Think

Young organizations and older organizations approach the challenge of establishing distributed teams from different sides, but they can struggle with it equally. They believe that having tools will solve the problem, but that's not the half of it. Tools are vital, but alone, they cannot complete the job. For example, some managers believe that going distributed means hiring people in India or Romania, who will work for less money. But that's not what going distributed means. Others think that setting people up with email or through a collaboration platform like Slack or Microsoft Teams makes them distributed. It doesn't.

The concept called distributed teams is a philosophy—an approach defined by a people-first, trust-heavy mindset that applies even when a team is physically dispersed, working from home or in satellite offices across the country.

Going distributed doesn't mean that people should never meet in person. In fact, later in this book, I talk about how necessary and enjoyable it is for distributed team members to meet together in person at least once a year.

Despite the fact that team members are all physically in different locations, it is my intention to highlight the importance of the human connection and face-to-face interaction whenever possible, to contribute to the shared trust mindset.

The future belongs to people and companies who are able to build human connectedness and collaboration into an optimized virtual environment.

Most importantly of all, going distributed gives you the foundation to manage a perpetually shifting landscape. The future belongs to people and companies who are able to connect those dots and build human connectedness and collaboration into an optimized virtual environment. It belongs to companies who can remain aware of the traditional arc of aging—from lean startup to bloated corporation—and navigate intelligently away from such choppy waters. It belongs also to those companies who learned from the global experience called lockdown, just how well the distributed teams concept can work, and just how well suited it is for this new digitally connected era.

Key Takeaways

- Teams consist of people who can share one heart and one vision.

- Building teams requires an ability to navigate by connecting the dots.

- The old approaches to management and to a company's life story are now being replaced by a technique that was field tested during the 2020 lockdown.

Offshore, Inshore, Nearshore, Remote, and Distributed

The terms that describe the ways people work off-site are sometimes used interchangeably and incorrectly. Developing an accurate and effective distributed teams model starts with clear definitions.

Offshore

How many times have you heard the term *offshore* used in a business context? For most people, it connotes work being done for a company, but being performed somewhere else in the world, usually where labor is cheaper—a manufacturing plant in China, for example, a call center in the Philippines, or a tech support center in India. It is a term that is often misused and misunderstood.

© Alberto S. Silveira Jr. 2021
A. S. Silveira Jr., *Building and Managing High-Performance Distributed Teams,*
https://doi.org/10.1007/978-1-4842-7055-4_3

By the way, I **was** one of those offshore people. Earlier in my career, while still living in Brazil, I wrote code. I was one of those "cheaper" coding people who do all that piecework, assembling and testing code for all types of programs and applications. I built what I had to build but had no knowledge of the company's North Star vision. I experienced no connection with the overall mission, the users, or the team. My manager would say, "Here's the code you need to write," and without the opportunity to ask questions or communicate with others in the company, I would write code using what little context I had. This meant that I, and all the other offshore people to this day, will do what is required, but it is done in darkness. Sometimes, for some industries, that's all you need. But other times, it causes more problems than it solves.

Offshoring vastly predates the distributed teams model. Most of the companies I consulted to or worked for had an offshore presence and would send product engineering work such as coding, architecture, product design, as well as customer support operations to countries on the other side of the world.

Sometimes, as I said, that is all you need. A room full of people gutting fish or assembling running shoes needs little shared vision. It is piecework, mindless, and detached from the end product and is often forced upon people with little means and even less choice. People can be trained to do this single task and are employed to do it as fast as they can for their entire shift. It is not the type of work that anybody really wants, which is why it has largely drifted away from more prosperous countries.

As a software engineer, I have worked with teams all over the world, in everything from small startups to enterprise-level organizations, in telecom, finance, healthcare, education technology, and marketplace. One of the things I observed regularly was how so many of these companies that embraced the traditional model of industry, including development, manufacturing, marketing, sales, and support, transferred so much of that work offshore.

Getting close to their processes allowed me to observe and analyze them from an engineer's perspective. From that viewpoint, it became easy to see how organizations that maintained geographically and culturally dispersed workforces often endured disconnects that were at odds with the promised cost savings. The offshoring of strategic activities such as building digital products can be a shortsighted move when it is approached from that singular cost savings perspective.

The Hidden Costs of Offshoring

Skilled or semiskilled work performed in foreign countries might make it appear that the direct cost is cheaper than back at home. But when you add the full seat cost together with the inevitable compromises in collaboration and context, you have to ask yourself, "Is that really cheaper, in terms of its return on investment (ROI)?"

I am not suggesting that professionals in traditional offshore countries like India or China are less intelligent or less capable than those in so-called wealthier countries. No country has a monopoly on innovation or excellence. But there are problems with communication and collaboration, including time zones and language—not only internally between layers of the organization but also externally with regard to fully understanding the customer perspective or user base.

It really helps when the teams behind the product understand the culture and the context of the market in which that product is being used. If a smartphone company is headquartered in the United States and offshores coding work to India, it makes sense to have a team located in India to support the customer base in that region. But this India-based offshore team cannot and should not be expected to fully understand the cultures and nuances of other parts of the world. This goes for any team and any country. You have to live there to get it.

This is why it is so difficult to establish high levels of performance in teams that are offshored. They are cut off from the context of the product, its overall market, and proactive team dynamics. Although the product being produced offshore might appear standard, whether it's code for a smartphone's OS or frozen fish sticks, there are significant geographical and cultural differences throughout the global marketplace that make the product and its production far from uniform.

Let's imagine you want to hire an engineer for your project. How much would it cost to hire a qualified engineer in the United States? For simplicity's sake, let's say $100,000 per year. In a less wealthy country, you could probably hire one for $20,000. That means you could get five offshore engineers for the price of one local engineer. At first glance, that makes sense on paper, and it would lead you to expect five times the productivity, since you're getting five offshore engineers for the price of one domestic one.

But in most cases, you would be wrong. I have seen it many times. I have worked for a number of international banking, telecom, and IT companies who have all done this. They all thought they were getting a deal. They weren't. Not because the engineers were necessarily bad, but because the context was wrong.

Pretty soon, the leaders who undertake this type of high-level offshoring realize they need a domestic redo. The quality, collaboration, and the *One Team, One Heart* spirit don't align with expectations. In fact, I have never met a leader that has said, "I am happy with the overall results from my offshore team." Instead, they say they are happy with how inexpensive they are, and some will go to the mat to defend that decision.

These leaders are often so distracted or even mesmerized by the idea of cutting costs, they don't see what's actually happening. They don't realize a cardinal rule that applies to high-performance teams just as it does for boat crews: to build a great product that is agile and innovative, you need more than just the ability to do a task; you need collaboration. People must be able to work together. Not as side-by-side names on a spreadsheet, but **together**, in real time and organically. Offshore work tends to lack this.

The Offshoring Disconnect

The prefix "off" should really drive this home. The "off" in offshore means the people, as good as they might be, are essentially severed from the project. Despite the undeniable quality of engineers and other professionals around the world, the likelihood remains: without effective collaboration and communication, when I ask you to do A, you'll end up doing B, even when you agree to A or even if you think you are doing A.

In addition to job or task definitions, there are significant cultural differences that must be considered. These can include time availability in relation to local and religious holidays, familial and societal traditions, laws, and other sensitive issues.

As a single example, I learned the hard way about the sensitive cultural differences that can occur between international peers when I went to speak at a tech-sector conference in Bangalore. India is, of course, a world leader in high tech, and my audience consisted of highly educated professional people. Unfortunately, part of my presentation used a project management model—one that I describe in more detail in Chapter 12 called *Elephant Carpaccio*. Needless to say, it did not go well.

In short, Elephant Carpaccio represents a technique of slicing a large project into more manageable components. Culturally, though, especially in Western countries, we look upon the elephant as a metaphor for a large and seemingly unmanageable project. Unfortunately, I was not aware of just how revered the elephant is in India. In Hindu culture, the elephant is sacred—a living incarnation of the deity Ganesha. It is not to be toyed with, especially in an analogy that includes slicing one up.

I should have known better. But this is what I mean by cultural differences. Indian engineers are just as excellent as their American counterparts, but when it comes to building the team, there are many obstacles that have nothing to do with the blueprints or code that the project is based upon. I should have known more about the culture of the country I was about to visit. To me Elephant Carpaccio was a turn of phrase, and to be honest, "elephant" was just a word. But it impacted my credibility and value in the eyes of my hosts, and even though this was a one-off event among peers, it is easy to see how such reverberations could last if I were trying to build a team of Indian engineers for offshoring.

Inshore

Because offshoring is not entirely conducive to building high-performance teams due to its multilevel lack of context, the next option is to bring the strategic elements of your business back to your home country, where connectivity and collaboration are more feasible, thanks to centralized office space and improved techniques for meeting in person and communicating online. This is what I refer to as *inshoring*.

But inshoring means hiring employees in the same country that you live and work in, which inevitably means factoring in its cost of living, which adds significantly to production costs.

"Wait a minute," you might say, "isn't inshoring just the act of hiring locally, like normal?" Yes, it is, if that's how a company started out—by hiring locally and not offshore. When I think of inshoring, I am picturing an activity where a company pulls back its outsourced work, back to its home country. So the jobs were "out there," and now they want to bring that work back home, inshore. If they hadn't offshored to begin with, they wouldn't have had to inshore later.

In many cases, despite their desire to hire locally from the get-go, many companies have no option but to offshore the lower-skilled components such as piecework assembly while inshoring the highest-value employees—executive level or extremely and uniquely skilled—whose costs can be amortized through the sales of the end product.

So, while it might be advantageous to retain the upper levels of a team inshore, in close cultural proximity, and perhaps send your raw materials and assembly components offshore, there remains a middle layer of professionally skilled people who cannot be commoditized to a point where they can be offshored, but who are too expensive to stay inshore.

So where does that leave you? Nearshore.

Nearshore

Leaders are increasingly starting to recognize the benefits of hiring nearshore, which is, from a geographical planetary perspective, about longitude rather than latitude. On a map, the lines of longitude run vertically from pole to pole, whereas the lines of latitude run horizontally, parallel to the Equator.

Moving manufacturing to China is a horizontal activity. Beijing, for example, is roughly the same latitude as New York City, but it is 12 hours apart in terms of time zones. Working with a China-based office involves some significant logistical challenges to the establishment and maintenance of high-performance teams, primarily the simple physical reality of living on a huge, round planet. Technology can send your face and your voice to Beijing in milliseconds, but the 12-hour time difference cannot be changed.

To help counter these challenges, the nearshore concept looks at geographic verticals that align with the north-south lines of longitude. These significantly help eliminate serious time zone differences. Most South American, Central American, and Caribbean countries sit roughly in the same vertical space as the United States. There is only one-hour time difference between New York City and Rio de Janeiro, for example. Much of the African continent sits directly below Europe, and Asia's economic centers, including the Philippines, South Korea, Japan, and China, sit in the same longitudinal space as Australia.

With this longitudinal alignment comes a degree of cultural connection. For example, many of the countries that share longitudes with the United States also share cultural similarities, including foods, music, and societal structure, as well as those that affect communication and collaboration more directly, such as gender dynamics and social hierarchies.

I may be generalizing somewhat here, but when there is some shared understanding of culture, this allows for greater human collaboration. Indeed, there is also much cultural connection between the United States and Europe, but when you do the math in terms of ideal working relationships within time zones, the combination of cultural and longitudinal similarity offers greater potential for working well together while allowing these professionals to thrive in their home countries, if they prefer, interacting with and empowering their local networks and economies. While some people enjoy moving to a new country to work and prosper, others, who have felt compelled to do so through lack of choice, may truly enjoy the double benefits of working with an organization located in another country while being able to stay close to home and family.

The time zone accessibility and cultural compatibility that nearshoring offers actually help encourage a third vital element, which is diversity. When people are colocated in the same close geographical area, as they would be when they are inshored, the working culture can become somewhat homogenized, even when the employees themselves are from diverse backgrounds. It's just a factor of living together in the same part of the world. You can't help but see and experience the same things at the same time. I find that by contrast, nearshoring strikes an ideal balance: there is greater compatibility and a comfort in terms of time zones, yet there are enough differences to keep a strong sense of diversity.

There will also be some restrictions—social, political, governmental, and practical—that will impact the development of nearshore teams. Brazil, for example, has labor laws that make it complicated to hire individual contributors directly without local representation—a partner who understands the local market, local and international taxes, laws, and regulations and social economic conditions in the country where you will be hiring expertise. Even within the United States, labor laws differ from state to state. These laws do not make the nearshore teams concept impossible, but it is more achievable when you have partners who understand the markets and the rules. I have experienced the success of this first-hand.

Offshore, Inshore, and Nearshore, and Their Relationship to Remote and Distributed

To this point in this chapter, I have described three types of working relationships—offshore, inshore, and nearshore. They are defined primarily by geography, economics, and level of contextual connectedness. In summary:

- Offshore work is usually far away, where labor is cheaper and where there does not need to be much context. Workers just write the code or assemble the parts with no need or opportunity to connect to the company or its North Star.

- Inshore work is done in a company's home country, perhaps at the main building, a satellite office, or even work from home. In this latter case, work from home does not automatically define an employee as remote or distributed, as I am about to explain.

- Nearshore work serves as an ideal option for the middle stratum of workers who require cultural connectedness and who may prefer to live in their home country and who can take advantage of time zone similarities.

The next two concepts, remote teams and distributed teams, have as their key identifying trait that the workers work outside of a company's official brick-and-mortar place of business. So what's the difference between remote and distributed?

Remote

Technology, especially in the area of video chat and document sharing, has come a long way in recent years, and as I have mentioned, and as you have likely noticed, prior to the significant disruptions of the 2020 lockdowns, some employers were already testing out the concept of having employees work remotely.

After all, it was intriguing to think a person could join a meeting from their home office, coffee shop, airport departure lounge, or anywhere that had decent Wi-Fi and a quiet place to sit down. And from joining a meeting, it started to become apparent that people could do more than just join meetings—they could do pretty much all of their work from somewhere other than a cubicle in the corporate office.

The apparent advantages of remote work are many. There's no need to commute to the office. Meetings and self-directed tasks can be done from a more comfortable place. There is less risk of running late due to travel delays. Video chats allow the benefit of seeing people's faces and reading body language, delivering greater context and emotional connection. Even though people survived quite well with telephone-based meetings for the best part of a century, video adds more depth, and besides, the younger generations of employees and managers who grew up fully immersed in visual media, quite rightfully, will accept nothing less.

But there's something "off" about the remote model *per se*, and the problem is right there in the name. A person who is remote is often not truly involved or engaged in the atmosphere of the workplace. They can be patched in temporarily, but they are not truly *there*.

A person who is remote is often not truly involved or engaged in the atmosphere of the workplace. They can be patched in temporarily, but they are not truly *there*.

In most meeting rooms, for example, there is a focal point for ideas—it might be an easel with paper, a dry-erase board, or a smartboard. This is a place where teams can add or address ideas with ease, and they can do so together, in the same space. It's the focal point of any truly effective meeting, the place where ideas are turned into tangible concepts or plans that in turn leverage the talents of all the people present. It's where brainstorming, problem solving, and design thinking thrive. It's where ideas beget further ideas, starting with conversation, soon to be wrestled into logical order. But to truly benefit from this, you have to be in that room.

Most of that synergy is consequently missed by someone connecting remotely. When one person is dialing in to a meeting room where all the other attendees are actually in that room, that remote person will not experience it in the same way, meaning they can neither contribute to it nor draw from it the same way. This person will also miss out on impromptu side conversations, at the table or in the hallway. Comments, gestures, even the simple raise of an eyebrow can change the course of a decision or team alignment. There are often additional conversations that occur after the remote call gets disconnected. That person is *remote* in the bad sense of the word. They are an outpost, never an integral part of the event.

Remote only works well when everyone is remote, and when everyone is remote, that becomes the starting point for building a high-performance distributed team. When every person in the meeting is calling in from somewhere, and where there is no central meeting room and no central whiteboard, the dynamic shifts from centralized to distributed. But when you have some people who are remote and some who are in person, it invariably becomes an unbalanced misaligned event.

Remote only works well when everyone is remote. When everyone is remote, they become distributed.

The shortcomings of being remote have more to do with reflecting on what actually makes a great, high-performing team. You cannot recreate the human sense of togetherness and presence from a remote location if the rest of the meeting attendees are together in a central office, even with all the best tools and gear. There needs to be a better way—one that capitalizes on improved communication technology, but which removes the social inequality of remoteness. It's not a matter of replication or lift and shift of office processes into the work from home space. It's a matter of redefining them for a new environment by removing its center. That's what the distributed teams model does.

The Distributed Teams Model

The distributed teams model leverages the benefits of inshore, nearshore, and remote while eliminating many of their shortcomings. The key identifying factor of a distributed team is that all its members are located in places other than a central office space. A distributed team means people are truly and clearly sharing the same collective goal from wherever they are. It's about inclusion, with all team members keeping constant sight on the North Star and none experiencing the contextual isolation of remoteness. The primary mission of the distributed team must be a blend of

- Hiring the best talent regardless of where they are located
- Establishing and maintaining cultural alignment

- Fostering and encouraging strong streamlined collaboration
- Demonstrating a tangible and beneficial return on investment
- Sharing the same collective goals
- Decentralizing the "source of power" that a boardroom or building represents

The distributed teams model (Figure 3-1) follows up on my previous comment that remote teams do not work well when just *some* of the team members are remote, but they do when *everyone* is remote. When everyone is remote, the word *remote* becomes moot. The team members have become distributed. Access to information and collaboration is the same for everyone. This setup negates the need for a geographic center, which is why the term *distributed* makes more sense. No one is actually remote and isolated from the group anymore. Everyone is where they are, distributed across the landscape, and on an equal footing.

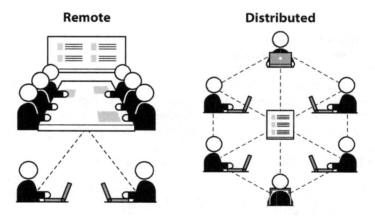

Figure 3-1. Remote vs. distributed

Whereas the word *remote* connotes a situation of loss or deprivation, as in being disconnected or cut off from the main place, the word *distributed* is empowering and highlights a strength that comes from connecting and meeting together across distances and in an egalitarian way. This goes a long way, not just in terms of direct, immediate, project-specific collaboration, but also in aligning with the North Star.

Throughout my career, a significant part of my work has always focused on bringing self-awareness to people and helping teams build a better distributed culture. I typically like to highlight changes in traditional office habits that can bring efficiency and inclusion to distributed teams. These include

- Using shared screens and collaboration areas that every team member can see

- Respecting time for focused, self-directed work activity (see Chapter 8) and ensuring that the common meeting times are balanced against it

- Communicating regularly on casual, non-work-related issues, to maintain a sense of community and social connection

- Maintaining connectivity by ensuring everyone has access to reliable high-speed Internet connection

- Adding photos to avatars and encouraging use of cameras during meetings to ensure team members have faces to relate to

- Running inclusive meetings where no people are left behind due to small snafus like a missing video chat link

- Remaining aware and respectful of time zone and cultural differences and factoring them into meeting schedules and available time blocks

- Providing stipends for home-based team members to buy snacks, lunch, or happy hour drinks, to maintain the same type of team bonding as they would enjoy at the office, especially in the nonformal drop-in spaces that I mention in Chapter 11

One aspect of remote and distributed workplaces that I am also very passionate about is the fact that it opens up more opportunities for people with disabilities, for instance. This is what equal opportunity means to me. I can bring people to the team based on who they are and what they can offer and feel no different than anyone else regardless of their geographical location. Over the years, I have been able to hire great engineers who have mobility issues for whom a daily commute to and from our midtown New York office is inconvenient and time-consuming.

Obviously, the additional benefits and how-to's about building and managing distributed teams will be discussed in all of the chapters in this book.

Can the Distributed Teams Model Apply to Offshoring, Inshoring, and Nearshoring?

Since the distributed teams model is, at its core, a centerless working community located away from the main corporate office, it is possible for all three models to learn and apply many of its practices and principles, but ultimately, this will depend on contextual elements, including a team's geographic location and relationship.

For teams who were traditionally offshored, the distributed teams model is unlikely to be successful. The most obvious reason is the time zone issue mentioned earlier. It could be conceivable for offshore colleagues to work asynchronously or even connect live at select times of day. But given that Beijing and New York City are 12 hours apart, it might be possible for team members to meet live at 8 o'clock, for example. It's an early morning meeting for one group and an evening meeting for the others. But this would not be optimal, not long-term, anyway.

Secondly, the nature of the work that offshore and nearshore teams perform does not really yield itself to the distributed teams culture. Even with Internet technology, there would be a disconnection or a gap between day-to-day activities, the communication, documentation, and alignment with the end user. It would still be difficult for the offshore team to see who is doing what work and who the customers are.

Ultimately, it might depend on the product, on a case-by-case basis. A company might send parts of its product to India or South America, for instance, but what is central to the distributed teams model is the need to treat people as part of the team. If you only hire someone across the ocean for the fact that they are less expensive, it will break the alignment with the North Star. It breaks the One Team, One Heart spirit.

In terms of nearshore countries, it is totally possible to create high-performance teams. I have done this already with team members distributed between the United States and Brazil, so I know it can work. The cultural alignment, similar time zone, shared guidelines, common focus on the end user—these are all vital to achieve what is needed to build high-performance distributed teams. As I have already described, it is more difficult to try to mix people from the United States with people across the Atlantic because you lose some of that cultural alignment and the time zone challenges are significant. But nearshore on a north-south alignment works great.

Of course, it is also eminently practical and highly advisable to apply the distributed teams model to employees who work inshore as well. This book is about the fact that people need not commute to a single location to get their work done efficiently nor do they have to feel remote when they patch in from their homes or from a satellite office, even if they work in the same state or municipality as the head office. That really is the point.

The key component of distributed teams is found in the One Team, One Heart concept, meaning there will be no walls between team members. Everyone is in the same boat, sharing the same collective goal, sailing toward the same North Star.

Should Everyone Vacate the Office and Go Distributed?

I don't think so. I think that the years and decades that we have built around the office-based work environment will not and cannot vanish completely. There is still a need for a brick-and-mortar existence, and I have no issue with that. It would go against human nature for everything to be completely and universally virtual.

There are also many good things about the office structure. Even though some workplaces have become tedious, it is unrealistic to consider an organization having no physical presence whatsoever. The distributed teams model is a great addition to a corporate presence, allowing people from different areas to collaborate and grow with the organization. The point always of the distributed teams model is not to say that everyone should go that way, but instead to show that it is a new and wholly viable variant on work and productivity, now made physically possible by high-bandwidth communication technology. It is a new option, but if chosen, needs the team structures described in this book to ensure it functions at its optimum.

The physical office will continue to exist. The social and tangible aspect flavor that the brick-and-mortar office space brings is undeniably important. But what might change is the roles of larger work centers like Manhattan, where I've dedicated the past decade of my life. So will those of São Paulo, Silicon Valley, Tokyo, London, and many other big centers around the world. Some people will continue to find ways to do their jobs from anywhere now that it has been proven possible. They have tasted this new lifestyle, and many will flock to it at least some of the time.

Another component that will change is the traditional nine-to-five office hour mindset. As I will describe later, this has never been as productive as we have been led to believe.

The distributed teams model brings with it a new outlook that will be better able to leverage the best from each person and each situation. That's a big change, and it's already happening. We have crossed that equator.

What About Freelancers and Contractors?

The distributed teams model need not be exclusive to full-time or part-time company employees. It can also include freelancers and contractors, whom I prefer to call *third-party partners*. I talk more about them in Chapter 10, but in brief, it's important to recognize the growing proportion of the workplace that is now made up of *third-party partners*. They add a particular type of expertise and benefit to a team due to their flexibility, the fact that they are available to add additional capacity, without the additional baggage of benefits, insurance, and taxes (they take care of these themselves), and are as professionally responsible for adding value to the team as any other full-time person.

Summarizing the Distributed Teams Concept

A distributed team is a redefinition of the work relationship between diverse teams and their employers that is based on geographical distribution, often across multiple regions and different countries. It offers flexible *work from anywhere* policy and establishes guidelines and rules designed to maximize collaboration, keep a high team morale, and increase efficiency. It caters to the changing demographics of work and capitalizes on new collaboration technologies to effectively replace the traditional meeting rooms and physical requirements of earlier decades.

The model reflects the growing future of work mindset, in which increasing numbers of qualified professionals seek a job or a profession that is more in line with their other life demands, which might also include additional time for family, education, and health, and in which technology becomes the primary channel of connection.

It is an opportunity for a new approach to work, one that could not have existed even a few years ago when Internet connections were not powerful enough to deliver video chat and large files with ease. Whereas the technologies of that time allowed for a certain amount of communication, what we now have is the opportunity for greater collaboration.

It is likely this will grow even further in the years to come, as virtual reality and augmented reality technologies make the centerless collaborative workplace more realistic, a far cry from the head-and-shoulders video chat screens that we currently use.

Earlier, I described how early motion pictures and TV shows were simply stage plays captured on film. So, too, these early years of the distributed teams workplace are using what people are most familiar with—the talking heads style of TV news and the formalized boardroom meeting behaviors captured and delivered through 2D video chat. But as anyone who has experienced immersive gaming knows, virtual reality is a transformative experience, and it is already being used in a wide variety of industries, especially for training.

Soon, it will cross its own equator into the workspace, just like computer software, smartphone apps, Facebook, Instagram, and TikTok all did, and with it will come an immersive 3D experience that will truly make any downtown boardroom sterile and antique.

The distributed teams concept is as new to many managers today as television was to our grandparents (or their parents). But it is a growing and extremely viable approach to work and equally importantly to the sense of community that is at the heart of an organization.

Key Takeaways

- Offshoring, inshoring, and nearshoring refer to the physical proximity of employees to a company and also to the degree they are contextually connected.

- Remote work refers to one person connecting to a group who is together elsewhere and has a tangible sense of being "outside the loop."

- The distributed teams model represents a place where no one is remote because there is no center. Workers are physically distributed across the map, but are fully immersed and connected to culture and context.

Seeking the North Star

If you get a chance to take some time to look at the night sky, when the air is clear and there are no clouds and especially when there is no moon, you will see a blanket of stars—an awe-inspiring display. The further you get from the lights of a city, the more it reveals to you. It is a truly amazing experience when you get to see the Milky Way for the first time, a hazy but unmistakable cloud that is our actual galactic neighborhood. In these dark nights, some of the stars actually reveal their colors—faint hints of blue, green, gold, or red.

Star watching is one of the lesser mentioned benefits of boating, since it allows you to push the bright city lights past the horizon, leaving you with vast blackness above and below.

It doesn't take long to learn the major constellations, and if you get a chance to watch the night skies regularly, over weeks and months, you will start to see the constellations pass slowly overhead. In the Northern Hemisphere, for example, the summer sky is dominated by Ursa Major, the "Big Dipper," while during the winter months, Orion the hunter holds court.

Mariners and farmers have watched these constellations for thousands of years—a mere blink of an eye in cosmological time—and they have all noticed how they appear to revolve around an "axis." That axis is marked by Polaris, the North Star.

© Alberto S. Silveira Jr. 2021
A. S. Silveira Jr., *Building and Managing High-Performance Distributed Teams*,
https://doi.org/10.1007/978-1-4842-7055-4_4

The position of Polaris in the northern night sky is in line with the Earth's axis of rotation. That is why the other constellations appear to revolve around it. They don't really, but it's an illusion that comes from sitting on a rotating planet in a rotating orbit in a rotating sky. Because of all of this, the North Star, officially called Polaris (the pole star) by Western astronomers, appears constant. This makes it an excellent tool for celestial navigation.

Throughout the centuries, sailors and explorers relied on its constancy to triangulate their position on the ocean, and even though we now use GPS for this purpose, astronauts, pilots, and sailors are all trained in celestial navigation as a reliable fallback. During the harrowing circumstances of the Apollo 13 mission ("Houston, we have a problem!"), the crew limped back to Earth with almost no battery power left. Their successful return was based in part on their ability to direct their vessel based on the stars that they could see from their windows.

In the summer, it is easy to find Polaris in seconds by looking for the unmistakable shape of Ursa Major, also known as the Great Bear, the Big Dipper, or the Plough (Figure 4-1). By drawing an imaginary line along the blade of the Plough and continuing through the sky, you will be able to find the next relatively bright star, which is Polaris. If you get to the big "W" of Cassiopeia, you have travelled too far.

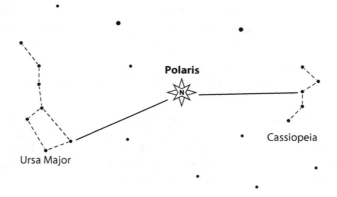

Figure 4-1. Locating Polaris

What is most interesting about Polaris, and something that makes it a powerful analogy in business, is that it is not the star's brightness that makes it a success, but its consistency. Other younger or larger stars like Sirius might outshine it in the night sky, but only Polaris can be consistently relied on for navigation.

The North Star in Business

Use of the term *North Star* in business took off during the period of incredible growth in Silicon Valley during the first wave of the computer/high-tech revolution of the 1990s. It has been used to represent and illustrate the consistent priorities needed for long-term sustainable growth. It helps also to reinforce the values built into a company's culture and products that in turn create value for customers and strategic direction for the company. The North Star should represent a company's "unwavering definition of its purpose," its products, its customers, and potential acquirers.

It's not a star's brightness that makes it a success, but it's consistency.

Why Is It Important to Have a North Star in Business?

Having a clear, consistent strategy with measurable goals and consistent core values is vital to an organization. You can't move forward if you can't identify your goal and your core values and if you can't verbalize both how and why you are going to pursue them. The North Star must be understood by everyone in the company. It should identify specifically what success looks like for your organization and should be easy and inspirational in its description. It should also identify a relationship between the needs of the customer, the solution that you plan to deliver, and the outcomes that you anticipate.

This definition becomes the guide, just like the North Star in the sky, that supports collaboration, reinforces trust, and delivers clarity for team members on what they need to accomplish, both individually and as part of the larger whole.

Once you have determined your North Star, you can turn to additional measurement tools and metrics to start identifying tangible goals and measuring progress. Some people call this the North Star Metric. I will discuss metrics in more detail in Chapter 7.

Your company's goal might be to grow to a sustainable level or to eventually get sold or acquired by a larger industry player. To me, selling your company is like getting a trophy. It's a reward. Someone is giving you something of value, including hopefully lots of money, for your hard work in building and steering the company to a place where its value is higher than your competitors.

In the centuries before GPS and radar, any crew that was setting out on an ocean voyage had to have someone on board who was intimately familiar with the art of celestial navigation—sailing by the stars. The parallels to maritime navigation and strategic business management are easy to see. As you crew your ship, you need to determine where you need to go (the New World? The Mediterranean? Around Cape Horn?), why you are going there, and what this is going to do for you, your crew, and your stakeholders and customers. The North Star in the sky serves as an essential guide to keep you and your vessel moving in the right direction and reorienting you when a storm blows you astray.

As a relevant aside, I mentioned Cape Horn because it is known as one of the world's most hazardous areas for ships to navigate due to strong winds, currents, huge waves, and icebergs. Portuguese sailors (part of my heritage) have historically been adept at navigating these types of seas, thanks to their exposure to the rough Atlantic off Portugal, especially the waves of Nazaré. This is another reason why it's important to think about pulling together a diverse crew for ocean-going vessels and distributed teams alike. You get a much greater diversity of experience, especially when you need it the most.

Even the term "orientation" has historical roots here. *Orient* is the Latin word for East, which referred to the rising of the sun, which is, of course, our closest and most important star. Not only was it vital to triangulate your location on the oceans by observing the North Star, an awareness of where the sun would rise on any given day of the year was also instrumental in figuring out where on the planet you actually were.

The East had enormous significance culturally and for religious reasons in terms of knowing where Jerusalem and Mecca were in relation to you. Following the establishment of the Silk Road, the spice trade and expanding commerce with Asian countries meant that knowing where *East* was was vitally important if you wanted to travel in that direction and equally important if you wished to travel in the opposite direction. The opposite direction—toward the West—was called *Occident*, referring to the setting sun. This was where the countries of the New World were to be found.

Some people see such historical stories and the words and symbols that we use in our language to be trivial and unnecessary, but there is a lot we can learn from history. People tend to do the same things over and over again, from generation to generation.

We tend to operate in cycles, economically, politically, and biologically, not only as humans but also as companies and cultures. The ideas of iteration, repetition, crossing the Equator, and making many trips around the globe, these are all reminders that we are on a continuous journey and it is up to leaders, as well as everyone else in the boat, to learn from the past and to find that focal point that serves as a guide to moving forward.

As just one example, much of the political reaction and social unrest that we have observed during the 2020 pandemic played out in exactly the same way in 1918 during the Spanish Flu outbreak. The dot-com bubble, the Bitcoin bubble, depressions, and wars, they have all happened before, just with different products and under different leaders. But it has all happened before. History can teach us much about our future.

> *If a man knows not to which port he sails, no wind is favorable.*
>
> —Seneca the Younger, Roman Stoic philosopher

Connecting the North Star to Distributed Teams

I find that my connection to the water and to the competition crews I sail with teaches me a great deal about how to plan for and work with distributed teams and how to identify the North Star. The questions I ask when setting up a team are aligned to those I would ask before setting sail with a regatta crew:

- Why are we doing this and why are we doing this now?
- How do we share the vision with everyone involved?
- How do we define success and what are we going to do to achieve it?
- Will the same thing that brought us here also bring us to the next level, or should we innovate at this time? If so, what are the risks?
- How are we going to differentiate ourselves from the competitors?
- What gaps do we need to address?

For almost every company and organization, the goal is to be successful, to some degree or other, but being profitable and sellable are not the primary components of the North Star. They are the desired results of a well-crafted North Star vision, along with closely followed metrics. They are a consequence of setting the right goals, and this starts and ends with the creation and management of a team.

Being profitable and sellable are not components of the North Star. They are the results of a great North Star vision.

Apple: "It Just Works"

Think about Apple. Why have billions of consumers loved Apple products to the point they buy from them repeatedly? In large measure, it's because they know that the products work, and their founder, Steve Jobs, knew to look beyond the boundaries of the conventional. He had the courage to follow his heart wherever it led, even if that meant breaking with traditional wisdom.

One of Apple's taglines was "It just works." The company always had great marketing and product management, especially under Jobs's guidance and vision. He was exceptionally good at communicating these to employees, contractors, and customers, not to mention the rest of the world.

In 1980, Steve Jobs identified Apple's mission, its North Star, as "To make a contribution to the world by making tools for the mind that advance humankind."

Although Apple today is a different organization than it was during both times Jobs was at the helm, his legacy of effective and genuine North Star–type vision statements is legendary. Perhaps my favorite is the tagline that Jobs used to introduce the iPod in 2001. The iPod was a portable MP3 player, one of many on the market in the time before the smartphone took over as a portable media center. While other MP3 player manufacturers touted how much RAM and storage space their device offered, Jobs skipped that and went straight to the vision statement: "1,000 songs in your pocket." This was a short phrase that addressed the only thing consumers would care about. Although you could consider this a marketing slogan, to me it embodies excellence as a North Star statement, as I think everyone involved in the design and testing of the iPods at that time could feel connected to its ultimate goal through this short phrase.

From Sea to Space

Sometimes, setting the goals means challenging a team to pursue unknown horizons or sail into uncharted waters. There may be no better current example of this than SpaceX, a rocketry company essentially brought into existence through the vision and contagious enthusiasm of its CEO, Elon Musk.

Basically, Musk turned the space transport business upside down, shifting it from a governmental science department like NASA and the Soviet/Russian space programs into an open source, distributed mindset, using new technologies and young scientists to create reusable rocket components, thus cutting the cost of each mission substantially.

From its inception, SpaceX employed a provocative fail-forward approach. Its teams shared a passion for achieving the seemingly impossible, such as landing and recovering the used rocket stages vertically on platforms that were floating on the ocean, so that they could be reused for future flights. They posted the landings—even the failures that fell off the barge and into the ocean—on YouTube, challenging viewers to come up with better ideas while still sharing their undeniable vision and passion for a new approach to space travel. This type of thinking was so out of the box, the older more established space transport companies found themselves facing more than just a new competitor. This was a new type of competition.

The vision that SpaceX holds is one of the best examples of aligning to the North Star that I have ever seen. Their North Star statement was (and still is as of publication of this book) this:

> *SpaceX designs, manufactures and launches advanced rockets and spacecraft. The company was founded in 2002 to revolutionize space technology, with the ultimate goal of enabling people to live on other planets.*

This is an inspiring and clear message that encapsulates the goals of the company, one that ensured that the right types of people—those who shared the spirit of that message—would want to work for SpaceX, no matter where they happened to be in the world.

The SpaceX North Star is not only a great statement, in my opinion, but it addresses the reality that to make significant change and progress, you have to challenge the status quo and be willing to move into uncharted waters, whether those are literal waters of the ocean, the vast gulfs of space, or, more likely for most of us, the equally uncertain worlds of business and technology.

All of these can be summed up in a simple quote from American author and professor John Shedd:

> *A ship in a harbor is safe, but that is not what ships are built for.*[1]

Business Is Much Like a Regatta

A regatta is a contest involving boats that go sailing around a course of buoys, or racing at speed, from point A to point B. In fact, the word *regatta* is the old Italian word for "contest." No matter how eager, passionate, and competitive they may be, the captains and crews of the competing boats do not set sail blind. Just like all mariners from centuries past and into the present, they make sure they know the coordinates and the challenges they may face, including wind, weather, and current. All of these need to be understood and prepared for.

---

[1]Shedd, John. (1928). *Salt from My Attic.* Mosher Press.

It's the same in business. We need to understand the market, its conditions and temperature, the competitors, trends, and other contributing factors. These are the elements that go into defining your North Star, and it's up to you as the leader to set those goals and get your crew aligned.

I consulted recently to a young tech company that was looking for navigational help. As I moved through the company, meeting people at all levels and observing their physical functionality, I found I had great difficulty identifying what their challenges were, let alone their solutions and plans.

I started by talking to product engineering, and then with the entire leadership team, but it became clear to me that they had not reached a level of maturity that would allow them to identify their North Star. They had succeeded in creating a product and they had a goal, but to me that was like having a boat in the water and a number that allowed them to enter a regatta. But they knew little about their competitors or the conditions, and even less about themselves.

Yes, they had built a successful product. But things move quickly, especially in software design, and their innovation lost its edge and they stagnated. They never connected with their North Star, and so their competitors caught up and overtook them.

I asked them, "What are you doing to ensure you stay better than your competitors? Does your team know where your North Star is? What are you doing differently? What innovation or actions are you bringing to future-proof your organization? What strategy tool, such as OKRs (Objectives and Key Results) or BSC (Balanced Scorecard), do you have that could actually lead your team to work toward its North Star?" But they had no answers. Their boat was rudderless. In fact, I felt that it had started to actually sink, right there in the middle of the regatta. There was water coming in and no one knew what to do.

The Three Pillars of a North Star

There are three key pillars needed to pursue a North Star. The first is to have an *established vision*. This means its leadership has defined the vision and has taken steps to ensure that the department objectives are connected throughout the organization.

The second must-have is establishing a collaborative team engagement, including *strategic planning and execution* across teams, ensuring full alignment. The collaborative exercise cascades down to each team, breaking down the larger company objectives into smaller objectives and measurable milestones without losing sight of the vision.

This can also be illustrated by looking at the opposite scenario: a situation of not having a collaborative team engagement. The result would be a top-down leadership strategy where teams would not be empowered to define milestones or set the coordinates for their own voyage. As a result, people's calendars would quickly fill up with status meetings, sync meetings, and other types of alignment meetings across teams—symptoms of a dysfunctional organization that typically lead to the culture of micromanagement.

This leads us to the third key element: a successful North Star process demands heightened *team autonomy*, which encourages and rewards self-accountability and proactivity. When the three pillars are present, it creates a model that empowers teams to be accountable since they will be measured by outcomes that demonstrate impact to the overall business rather than just the milestones given to them.

I like to refer to this model as the *collaborative team engagement model*. This model focuses on outcomes rather than simply using the "number of hours worked" as an indicator of productivity, which makes it easier to identify and work with KPIs (key performance indicators) such as revenue, NPS (net promoter score—a DevOps approach to essentially surveying and measuring user satisfaction), and ROI (return on investment).

Here's a software industry example. In a collaborative team engagement model, software delivery teams would be measured by uptime, MTTR (mean time to recovery, discussed further in Chapter 7), or NPS, described previously. In a noncollaborative team engagement model, delivery teams would simply be measured by story points delivered or the number of bugs fixed in a week, which provides static data but which cannot extend to a wider wisdom of the marketplace or team members' own roles within it.

The three components of the North Star must be crystal clear, addressing the coordinates and milestones that lead to the final destination, and those milestones must serve as checkpoints to ensure we do not lose sight of where we are trying to go. As each boat in the fleet takes its own journey toward the destination, the outcomes are measured consistently throughout the journey, and adjustments are made to the route as needed.

The Trust Mindset and the North Star

One of the biggest challenges when it comes to building teams and aligning them to your North Star is understanding the degree to which trust and empowerment must be present.

For local teams and for distributed teams alike, leaders must commit to a trust mindset and must demonstrate that trust consistently. As I mentioned earlier, many so-called leaders enjoy the psychological reassurance of seeing people in the office. They might not have clear goals or vision, but they feel good when they see people around, and they have faith that everyone is moving toward a direction. That's not trust—it's an act of self-comfort that is both incorrect and also gives little back to the employees themselves.

The fact that people are present in the workplace does not mean they are working in sync with the company's North Star. And that in itself is not because they are lazy. Most people are not lazy, but they might lack guidance and might be fearful to ask. They may be overwhelmed with conflicting priorities. They might lack sufficient motivation or clarity on what their individual and team goals are.

People in a workplace have to deal with a range of distractions and priorities that may either be invisible or seem important to a manager, but which nevertheless occupy their minds and their time to the detriment of everything else. These may come from inside the workplace or outside, in the form of emails, messages, and meeting requests. This is a classic time management challenge and has been for decades. Just because a person is sitting at their desk in their office does not mean they are getting the right work done or using their talents to maximum benefit.

Team members often get the blame for subpar performance, but in many cases, the problem lies with an upside-down work culture in which low-level priorities like email supersede higher tasks, time is wasted through bad habits, workdays are not aligned with individual employees' own circadian energy levels, and professional development education is delivered in an anachronistic overload style.

The manager has the ability to do something about it by connecting with each team member, helping guide each toward developing the skills, and leveraging the motivation that produces superior results. This is what alignment to the North Star requires, and I do not believe you need an office building for that. At least, not always.

I can't help but picture the captain of a large boat surveying the crew working hard on deck, even with someone on the tiller, yet with none of them having any idea or concerns about where they should be headed and what the conditions of the weather and water might be. So long as it appears that they are all moving, that's good enough, even though they might be moving in circles. Though this is a highly improbable scenario for any ship, it is actually highly likely within corporate teams.

How to Build Trust and Rapport

Is trust an emotion or a fact? Can you trust someone because you feel strongly that they are able to do a certain task or because you know they can do that task? This is a tricky question because most things in life fall neatly into one of these two buckets—you either feel it or you think it. Not so with trust.

Trust is a hybrid. You can only have positive, trustworthy feelings toward a person once you know enough about them to be able to feel positively about them.

Trust is also earned. It can take a long time—months or perhaps even years—to gain a person's trust, but it can take mere seconds to lose it, often forever. So it must be treated with absolute respect.

The steps to earning trust are all easy in theory, but they take diligence. You can earn a person's trust by being true to your word—doing what you say you will. Your actions are being constantly observed. A manager who says "We are all one big team" must prove this by giving team members the leeway and empowerment to take care of their work and their calendars and to communicate with each other. As the business expert (and former CTO of Rent the Runway and former VP of Technology for Goldman Sachs) once wrote:

> The bedrock of strong teams is human connection, which leads to trust. And trust, real trust, requires the ability and willingness to be vulnerable in front of each other.[2]

I would add to this that such bedrock must be available to all.

Trust is built by being transparent—no hidden agendas—and by being accountable. Great leaders earn trust by ensuring their team members receive credit for the victories, while the leader shoulders any blame or responsibility for failures or errors.

Trust is built by listening actively, by showing empathy and demonstrating genuine care by making available those most highly prized parts of the workday—your time and your attention.

Finally, in my opinion, the best way to build trust is to show trust in others.

A platform of trust and communication then develops rapport—the willingness to create a culture of easy communication and empathy, both work based and on a more social level. This can be done just as easily using video chat technology, for distributed teams, as it can for on-premises teams, both as group conversations and regularly scheduled one-on-ones. Maybe even more so, because of the way in which we are sharing our home space during these meetings, which might include living room backgrounds, kids, and pets. A manager who greets these very human parts of a video chat with warmth and who actually encourages it will immediately establish or reinforce trust and rapport by recognizing the humanness of teams and team members.

---

[2]Fournier, Camille. (2017). *The Manager's Path: A Guide for Tech Leaders Navigating Growth and Change.* O'Reilly.

Here's one of my favorite examples of leadership, which in its utter simplicity might show how trust and rapport can be established in small yet extremely powerful ways:

> *On a cold night, seeing a Secret Service agent standing guard outside the Oval Office, President John F. Kennedy asked him inside but was told he couldn't. So Kennedy brought out two cups of hot chocolate, which they both drank in the cold.* [3]

The Power of Empowerment

Empowerment is the ultimate demonstration of trust in a team member, and again when trust is demonstrated, so too is it earned. Employees thrive on the opportunity to stretch their skills, and they crave the acknowledgement of work well done, and they also crave feedback and learning opportunities. Empowerment gives employees the chance to make decisions, to learn, and to actually discover new and better ways of doing things—a direct dividend of—and a nod to—the continuous improvement culture that I discuss in more depth, in the following.

The "What Were You Thinking" Paradox

Here's what I call the "what were you thinking" paradox. Imagine a situation in which a team member is empowered to try something new, but makes a mistake and is called into the office to explain or perhaps is made to do so in front of the entire team.

A poor leader might chastise the employee by asking "What were you thinking?" a question that, when spoken aggressively, implies incompetence and poor judgment on the part of the employee.

A great leader might instead ask, "What were you thinking?" the very same words, but this time spoken with genuine curiosity and empathy, meaning "I would like to learn more about your approach and how you handled this. Your thoughts might reveal a better way that we can work on perfecting together. Please tell me more."

So the same words can be used to build trust and rapport, not only with this individual team member but throughout the entire team, who will all be observing this interaction.

---

[3]Beschloss, Michael. (2018). *Presidents of War: The Epic Story, from 1807 to Modern Times.* Crown Books.

To me, these are the actions of great leadership upon which great teams are built. When great teams are built and maintained in this way, the North Star becomes truly reachable.

One Last, Great Thing About a North Star, Especially for Distributed Teams

I started this chapter by talking about the night sky. It's the sailor in me. All sailors have an affinity for the sky as much as the sea. Because of this, I find the concept of a North Star to be very reassuring and calming through its consistency and its singularity, as I have just described.

But one of the other great benefits of the North Star as it applies to distributed teams is that stars are something we can all see, no matter where on the planet we are. People who live in the Northern Hemisphere can locate Polaris, the actual North Star. And even though Polaris is not visible in the Southern Hemisphere, people there can locate the Southern Cross, the center of which sits above the South Pole and serves a similar consistent purpose for human navigators. The point is the stars are far enough away to be a reliable point of reference to people, no matter how and where they are distributed on any part of the planet. I think that makes great sense and ties in well when considering the enormous potential of distributed teams, wherever their individual team members happen to be.

Key Takeaways

- A North Star is a message that connects people through a shared vision. It should be memorable and easy to understand.

- Although it is a simple message, a North Star requires the establishment of trust, rapport, and empowerment.

- In addition to its established vision, a North Star must address strategic planning and execution and team autonomy.

Finding Balance Through the Rule of Three

Before there was celestial navigation, there was the rule of marteloio, a technique applied by medieval mariners that essentially used compass markings and basic trigonometry to plot location and direction. This was an early version of triangulation, a term of wayfinding that takes readings from three known points to calculate location or distance. These are not old techniques lost forever in the mists of history. The mechanics behind the GPS app on your phone or the navigation system in your car is all about triangulation. It calculates your location by reading signals from a field of satellites parked in orbit around the Earth. It only needs to read the signals from three of these satellites to do the same thing medieval sailors did with compasses and sextants. Wherever you are on Earth, there are GPS satellites visible for your device to use.

The principle of working with items in threes has enormous value in numerous areas of life because "three" provides perfect balance. It is neither too much nor too little. As just one simple example out of many, a three-legged stool will always be stable, whereas a four-legged one will inevitably suffer from slightly different leg lengths or the unevenness of the ground.

© Alberto S. Silveira Jr. 2021
A. S. Silveira Jr., *Building and Managing High-Performance Distributed Teams*,
https://doi.org/10.1007/978-1-4842-7055-4_5

The Triangle of Project Management

Project management has been part of human endeavor for thousands of years. Even before people used that actual term, during the epochs that preceded the First Industrial Revolution, there were three distinct ages in which project management played a central role: the Stone Age, the Bronze Age, and the Iron Age. During each of these periods, long before engines, hydraulic power, or computers, people built roads and structures, harnessing raw materials, pairing muscle power with physics and human genius to create items that still exist today. To make this happen, they had to work to a plan.

The triangular relationship is used in project management to describe a project's central components: scope, time, and cost. Scope can be thought of as the overall "bigness" of the project, in terms of what the end product (the deliverable) will be and what will be needed to achieve it.

No project manager has a crystal ball. No one can truly predict the final cost of a project, but that's exactly why the practice of project management exists; that's its true value statement. Even though project managers can't predict the future, they can do the next best thing: they can write it, by factoring the scope, time, and cost triangle into a project plan.

A project plan is like the history of a project, written before it happens. By taking the time to make careful calculations, do adequate research, and factor in contingencies and fallbacks, a project manager can actually bring a project in and have it conform to the triangle of project management, not by chance, but by the opposite of chance: through effective planning and communication.

The Golden Triangle

Managers and leaders within companies will be familiar with another triangular relationship, that of people, processes, and tools. Sometimes called the Golden Triangle, it is used to illustrate to components of superior customer experience. The *people* concept connects employee engagement to the customer experience. The *processes* concept creates consistent procedures and eliminates wasteful habits. The *tools* concept identifies the devices used to make the connections, including technology and metrics.

The Triangle of My World: The Iron Triangle

For the types of teams and production requirements that I am used to in software development, we speak about the Iron Triangle as the triangular relationship that combines product management, product design, and engineering when building digital products.

Behind each of these terms, there will be a person or people who represent one of three specialized disciplines, whose outlook and experience hold the project and product together in perfect dynamic tension.

Product Management

The product manager is a person/group who is responsible for maximizing the value of features and products created by the specific delivery teams. To do this, product managers collate expertise from market analysts, business strategists, customer liaisons, internal stakeholder managers, researchers, product marketers, and project managers.

They focus on answering the Why and What questions, and the kinds of people who often join a product management group include product managers and business analysts.

It is important to highlight the maturity model at play here. Some product managers develop a strength initially in running projects (inbound), while others are great at connecting work to the market (outbound). Strong and more mature product managers should be able to do both, since they represent the connection between the inbound and outbound that is necessary for building great products.

Product Design (User Experience)

Software is useless if people cannot intuitively use it. Think, for example, about the ease with which an app downloads into your phone, ready for instant use. No matter how well it is coded, if the consumer doesn't get satisfaction within the first few seconds, they will discard it.

Product designers bring expertise in user research, information architecture, interaction design, visual elements, and creating documentation and specifications for projects and features. Designers work with the product management people to determine requirements and scope. They also work with the engineers to understand what is possible to build.

They focus on the Why and the How. Typically, the kinds of titles that work in the product design group include visual designers, user experience (UX) designers, design researchers, content strategists, and design ops.

Engineering

Engineers bring expertise in developing, designing, observing, automating, documenting, and testing the product. To do that, engineers work with product management to evaluate proposed technical solutions and scope, and they work with product design to provide feedback and iterate through proposed design solutions.

They focus on the How and the What. Typically, the kinds of titles that you see in the engineering organization include front-end/back-end development, quality assurance (QA), security, automation, architecture, cloud operations, and mobile specialists.

This group collaborates to design, test, and build a product that serves a purpose, works correctly, and can be used by end users.

The Dialog Box Conundrum

People who write code naturally have a different outlook than that belonging to an end user who is installing the software or downloading the app for the first time. A significant point of collision between these two worlds is the dialog box—that place where an end user is expected to issue a command to the software. In some cases, this can be confusing, for example, a dialog box that asks a user if they wish to continue with a command that will cancel a procedure. The dialog box might look like the one shown in Figure 5-1.

Figure 5-1. The dialog box conundrum

In this case, clicking OK will proceed with the cancelation of the installation, while clicking Cancel will stop the cancelation process. Obviously the verbiage for the end user is confusing, even though the code behind it would not be.

Everything that is produced for human usage, from physical objects to workspaces, has the potential to misalign when its design and development pass through a single channel. The point is, when design passes through only one mindset and through only one set of experiences, its odds of completely successful deployment are slim, hence the need for an Iron Triangle approach.

The Iron Triangle and Distributed Teams

For distributed teams, the concept of the Iron Triangle brings a balanced team formation and leadership. The three people from different professional perspectives together are constantly collaborating and are accountable for aligning team members and the day-to-day activities with the North Star.

There is a dynamic balance in using three people with different perspectives. The energy of creativity has its own momentum. A single person in charge would be like a single helicopter blade, which, if placed alone to rotate, would fly off and render the craft unusable. Three blades provide balance, allowing a central stability, with each blade rotating independently, with their collective momentum being held in balance and in check at the center point.

The dynamic tension of the three creates a balanced central point where better decisions can be made. I like to say that is one of the many manifestations of the *One Team, One Heart* principle, which helps teams speak the same language, see the same vision, feel the same spirit, and focus on the same outcomes. And to get to One Team, One Heart, you need a solid triangular support.

Traditionally we have referred to individual areas of the product engineering department as if they operated in isolation. It would be typical for someone to say "I have a back-end team" or "I have a quality assurance team" or discuss the responsibilities of the "release team." There's no question that it's good to have qualified people in those specialties, but, to build high-performance teams, you need people from all disciplines and specialties to think, feel, and act as a single unit.

When there is no Iron Triangle present, a product will end up representing the single person who made the decisions, and this generally results in failure, because the biases of one individual will fail to adequately account for any practical needs outside of their purview. It also tends to grow silos within organizations.

The Iron Triangle helps with the decision process to prioritize what delivery teams should be working on (I discuss delivery teams in more detail in Chapter 6), aligning strategic feature work and technical feature work with the single key criteria: to identify and understand the most important thing for the business that people should be working on. Some of the Iron Triangle goals are as follows:

- Leverage the strength of each team member's expertise and perspective.

- Create a team environment where all members share the responsibility of guiding solution execution.

- Provide an equal sense of ownership and accountability for solutions the team delivers, so that everyone owns success and identifies opportunities to improve.

- Ensure transparency about goals, objectives, and strategic vision across the team.

The key here is that for distributed teams, a collection of three minds or three domain experts is the optimum for balancing the leadership load and expertise inventory, without becoming cumbersome and top heavy.

Triangles Inside and Triangles Outside

The triangular relationship can be extended to cover both the inbound and the outbound sides of the process that ultimately delivers a product to the customer's hands. This creates a bowtie shape (Figure 5-2). Although it appears to break the rule-of-three motif, in fact, it does the opposite by keeping the number of people involved on either side to the same highly economic and practical number: three. Because inbound and outbound are substantially different yet tightly coupled, it not only makes sense to have a triangle for each, it also strikes a note of perfection to have them conjoined by the person who can operate in both: the product manager.

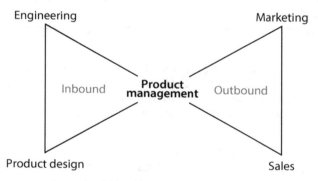

Figure 5-2. The bowtie of product management

Looking at this in terms of my world in the software industry once again, whether an enterprise or small organization, it is a place fraught with deadlines, security issues, feature requests, demand for innovation, quality concerns, and rapid change. It needs the Iron Triangle to ensure all bases are covered as the product rolls through the pipeline toward release into the world. Thus, the inbound process represented by product management, product design, and engineering needs a balanced outbound triangular relationship formed by product management, marketing, and sales. When connected, the two triangles create the solution needed to deliver the product to the customer.

As I have already described the roles of product management, product design, and engineering, here are the two other roles that drive the outbound process, roles that pretty much everyone in business is already familiar with: marketing and sales.

Marketing

The marketing team helps drive awareness and demand for the product largely by using various forms of media to connect with those who are in charge of purchasing the product. Marketing people must have an intimate knowledge of the product and of the marketplace in order to frame a message that will be attended to.

Sales

In any company, in any industry, the salespeople are responsible for getting the entire project over the finish line, building rapport with buyers, and overseeing the purchase agreements and encouraging long relationships with customers and prospects alike. Although the stereotype of the aggressive foot-in-the-door sales rep still persists, the golden rule of successful sales is to act as a trusted advisor rather than a fast-talker, and for this, a great sales manager must have a thorough understanding of each customer's needs, a willingness to listen more than talk, and a deep understanding of the product. Although marketing might move a customer from awareness to curiosity to desire, it is the great sales professional that transforms people's desire into commitment, and beyond, to becoming advocates for the brand.

In both the internal and external triangles, there may be many dozens or hundreds of people, but they are coordinated and motivated by a clean and functional trinity.

Driving the Iron Triangle Mindset in Distributed Teams

When people think about software design, they might naturally picture a few thousand designers working together on a large campus, like the ones at Google, Apple, and Facebook. But it is equally likely that many of these people are working in distributed mode. It's an industry perfectly suited for this, but it's not the only one.

Since there are many other lines of business that might be deploying or contemplating a distributed teams model, it is good to know there are a few straightforward guidelines that can help drive the Iron Triangle leadership concept forward and spread its message out across the distributed population.

The Iron Triangle is ultimately about team formation. Teams of all types depend on each team member to do their part. If you look at a soccer team, for example, the responsibility for success does not rest solely with the goalkeeper. Everyone, on and off the field, has a part to play. There are thousands of books, seminars, and motivational quotes about teams, of course, but one of the reasons there are so many is that the concepts of team are quickly forgotten once different personality types start to emerge and predominate. This is why constant reflection upon the nature of team as a concept is needed.

Communication among the members of the Iron Triangle must be streamlined (I talk about this in Chapter 8). The focus on the North Star must be sharpened across the entire team, with procedures established to ensure it is never lost. There must be a tangible atmosphere of trust and empowerment. As described in Chapter 4, trust is what fuels the spirit of collaboration, and empowerment helps widen perspective from "looking to solve problems" to building great products for the end users. Conversations should be shifted "to the left" where the three internal Iron Triangle components are aligned from the project idea to delivery.

For readers who do not work in software development, shifting to the left is a term used in software design culture—DevOps—and it means moving quality control earlier into the process. The shift represents the same type of change to an established culture as going distributed does—they are both in reaction to changing times, and both represent evolution and refinement of a production process.

For readers who do not work in software development, shifting to the left is a term used in software design culture—DevOps—and it means moving quality control earlier into the process. The shift represents the same type of change to an established culture as going distributed does—they are both in reaction to changing times, and both represent evolution and refinement of a production process.

The Rule of Thirds

The Iron Triangle concept is not a fad. As I have described, it is an optimized collection of talents that helps teams fulfil their responsibilities by balancing expertise in manageable and equitable proportions, based on the concept of "three."

It makes sense, then, given how important communication is to the act of leadership, to look briefly at the power of the threefold structure in the creation of clear messaging. Humans naturally respond to rhythm, and leaders have used this fact successfully throughout history. From lofty concepts such as "life, liberty, and the pursuit of happiness" through to more practical messages like the classic railroad crossing reminder, "stop, look, and listen," these phrases resonate with rhythm. When spoken, they are delivered with a percussive cadence that is highly influential to the human listener on more than just an intellectual level. They become tangible, connecting with our internal musicality in just the same way music and drumbeats do.

Consequently, great orators deliver passion and motivation through the cadence of their speech. Barack Obama, for example, Martin Luther King, Jr., and Winston Churchill—these are three leaders whose speeches were intended to be heard by millions of people as a powerful sound. You need to work with the natural rhythms of the body to connect with human sensibilities, and that is easier to do when the words are spoken or chanted, especially in a threefold cadence.

But spoken words are not the only rhythmic verbal tools at a leader's disposal. Bullet points in a memo or document, as humble as they may seem, are more likely to be read when there are just three of them. Similarly, an email is more likely to be read and acted upon if the entire message is no more than three paragraphs long (and short paragraphs at that). If you give people a list of things to do, anything longer than three items will be either forgotten or subject to procrastination. That's just how it is with people. The secret is to keep the rhythm and structure by sticking to a manageable rule of thirds.

TV shows, movies, photographs, and paintings often use the rule of thirds in visual composition. When done correctly, most viewers will not consciously notice, but it contributes to a level of viewing satisfaction and attention that is always the goal of producers and their stakeholders.

The Rule of Thirds for Boating

When it comes to boating safety, many boaters are recreational and not always up to speed with all the regulations, even though they should be. As such, it helps to keep messages short and memorable. One of these vital messages applies the rule of thirds quite literally. It states that one-third of a boat's fuel must be for the outbound trip and one-third must be for the trip back to harbor. This leads to the question, "What's the other third for?" The other third is the reserve.

Boating is a highly unpredictable activity, despite people's best-laid plans. Water and the weather above it can change in an instant. You might need to change course or use fuel to accelerate away from danger in a hurry. You might need to sail headlong into a strong wind or even go out of your way to assist a stricken vessel.

It would have been equally easy for the rules to say, "Make sure you have enough fuel for the unexpected!" or "Put more fuel in than you think you'll need!" but people's interpretations of these suggestions can be highly subjective, making them less useful and less memorable. When you describe a fuel tank in thirds, people can imagine it, and the message gets through more effectively.

The Iron Triangle and Leadership in Perspective

To put the Iron Triangle and the concepts of the rule of three into the perspective of leadership and of developing high-performance distributed teams, let's look at leadership itself. The process of leading a distributed team is not that different from that of leading a team of people inside one single office in one single building.

Leadership is a loaded term. It involves guiding people toward a goal while managing their individual needs. It means taking responsibility for team action while empowering team members to drive themselves. A leader must inspire confidence and demonstrate capability. Without leaders, people cannot move forward. If no leader is present in a group, one will naturally emerge. It is vital, and it is a force of nature.

To me, the best definition of a leader is "someone whom I want to follow and whom I choose to follow." That might sound overly simplistic at first glance, but think about it. A person could be a brilliant scientist or economist or programmer—and I could admire that person's skills, but would I want to follow them on a voyage? Maybe, but maybe not.

I might also know someone who was filled with all of those social-emotional talents such as empathy, diplomacy, compassion, and interpersonal communication, but would that person also have the navigation skills and experience to undertake a voyage? Maybe, but maybe not.

Leadership demands a combination of skills that some people possess innately and that others must learn. One of the best ways to identify the traits of a great leader is to think about someone you have encountered before, either in a work situation or someone in the public eye, who you think exhibits the qualities of a great leader, and then break this down, asking yourself what it is about this person that makes them so.

Very often the attributes of great leaders are consistent. A great leader exudes genuine confidence and a sense of destiny, is organized enough to make things happen, and can communicate well to those who follow. But beyond these practical components, great leaders never lose that common touch. They seem approachable, they demonstrate respect to everyone they meet, regardless of rank. Inasmuch as they are a leader, they still seem to be one of us. People who choose to follow a leader do so with trust as the chief connection point.

This is the cause of many problems in the traditional workplace and can be so in a distributed teams environment as well. When managers cannot delegate tasks, they demonstrate distrust of their team members. When they micromanage, they demonstrate distrust and simultaneously prevent team members from trusting them. An entire two-way street of trust is blocked. Much of the toxicity of the typical workplace stems from an atmosphere in which people sense they are not trusted or respected. These are all elements that help crush the positive energy that every team is capable of and have been the bane of corporate life for decades.

That's why my definition of a leader reads the way it does: "someone whom I want to follow and someone whom I choose to follow." The fact that I want to follow is an emotional response. The fact that I choose to follow is based on logic. I need both of these to establish trust, and so do you, and so do they.

What's the opposite of not having Iron Triangle leadership while building products? It reverts to the traditional—but not highly effective—way that many organizations have organized their teams over the years. This has often resulted in having a team organization where the decision-making process emanates from a single perspective. It goes back to the example of having a helicopter with one blade. It may exert energy and rotate, but because it is not balanced, it will be extremely difficult to get the vessel moving in the desired direction.

The Iron Triangle brings that balance by aligning different perspectives. It also brings an effective leadership model to teams.

The tension between the three sides is necessary and healthy for the creation of better products. It's a valid demonstration of the fact that tension and even mild conflict are not necessarily bad since they can lead to creativity. Without some degree of friction, innovation suffers. Fostering a creative and innovative mindset within the Iron Triangle is important, and people should feel comfortable disagreeing with each other.

This is a delicate topic that requires caution and diligence, which are fundamental elements of leadership. Conflict, like wind for sailors, has differing levels of benefit. No conflict or no wind means no progress. The right amount of either generates forward energy, even—and especially when—the team can move and adapt to its changing vectors. But too much wind can lead to boats getting into trouble, and for teams, too much conflict moves into that danger zone in which business processes are negatively affected, and formalized conflict management and resolution strategies must be deployed.

Ultimately, for teams, the idea is never to advocate for the creation of a purposefully tense environment, but rather one where people agree to disagree and strive to challenge the status quo, including the team leader's own ideas. This ultimately helps teams to keep a focus on their North Star.

Key Takeaways

- The power of three is highly practical in many areas including leadership, collective expertise, and effective decision-making.

- The Iron Triangle concept when extended to illustrate the full production cycle of a product forms a bowtie, but the concept of the triangle still rules.

- The Iron Triangle helps deliver a leadership model that brings balance, producing better outcomes.

Setting Sail

Building a Distributed Team Organization

I love to crew on large sailboats—40 feet or larger. I like specifically to sign on as a crew member and participate in regattas. One that I regularly return to takes place off the coast of Croatia in the Adriatic Sea. This is an exciting place to sail. The Adriatic is the northernmost arm of the Mediterranean Sea and has Croatia, Montenegro, and Albania on its eastern edge and Italy to the west.

The regatta involves a number of professional sailors who come here to race on their vacations. It lasts seven days, and there are two or maybe three races each day. Of course, much depends on the weather. Too much wind is as bad as no wind.

I am a crew member, not a captain. The captain of our boat is actually an Olympic medal winner, so I would say he is very well qualified for the role, and that's why I trust his command. The whole crew meets in the morning to define the route and to identify our North Star. My job is to check the

© Alberto S. Silveira Jr. 2021
A. S. Silveira Jr., *Building and Managing High-Performance Distributed Teams*,
https://doi.org/10.1007/978-1-4842-7055-4_6

equipment and lines (ropes) and to make sure everything I need is in place. I also help in the team effort to make the boat as light as possible by determining what we can safely leave behind.

My position is at the front of the boat (the bow), and when wind conditions blow from the stern, which is not ideal, I must fly the spinnaker, a large, special-purpose, and rather unwieldy sail that is flown only in these conditions. It takes a certain amount of training and aptitude to be able to fly one efficiently, because time is of the essence and the physics are rather complicated. Most of the crew speaks Hungarian, which I do not. But we have worked out a streamlined communication process to ensure that when they call for the spinnaker, even in their Hungarian accents, I know my job is to pull it and fly it right away so that we can turn (jibe) through the wind.

On the water, there are moments where we are extremely busy and others where our job is just to sit on the side of the boat as a counterbalance to the force of the wind, which can tip the boat substantially to one side. That's what being part of the crew is all about.

Every night we pull into a different port, and as I mentioned at the start of this book, as much as it may be a thrill to head out of a harbor to start an adventure, it's also a wonderful sensation to come back to a safe port to rest.

When we get to the harbor, not only do I talk with the rest of my crew (thankfully, the Hungarians can speak some English) but I also talk to other crews from other boats—especially to the person who has the same job that I do. This type of interaction helps me to understand why it's so vital for the work process to be divided up into teams and squads, overseen by a captain, held together by a streamlined communication process, and driven by passion.

On a racing boat, it is common for the captain to share key responsibilities with senior crew members. On larger vessels such as freighters or navy ships, this is a given.

Building a Cohesive Organizational Structure

When you watch a movie that involves a fleet of ships going out to battle regardless of the era, the visual impact is always the same: a large group of vessels of different sizes, with different specialties, heading out in formation with a singular purpose—a clearly understood North Star (Figure 6-1).

Figure 6-1. Moving toward a single North Star

These vessels are working in consort—each has a specific role to play in support of the mission. They are a cohesive organizational structure, but at the same time that they are members of this group, they are also individual vessels, each with a captain and a crew, and within the crew there are further subsets—teams of specialists. These teams may have unique abilities and missions of their own, but at the same time, they will share particular abilities with other teams.

There's nothing overly complicated about this. It's visible when you drill down from the bird's-eye view of the entire fleet, to observe the workings of a single ship.

I think of this when I think of the various distributed teams that I have set up and overseen. They still have relationships, specialties, and cross-team connections that must be planned, communicated, and deployed. They must be created and managed to handle the current demands of an organization, but they must also be able to scale up and scale down without impact on outcomes, and that's worth mentioning here. When a company faces significant growth, it is easy for it to lose track of the key elements that contribute to high performance. It's common, for example, for companies that perform very well when their size is around 10–15 people to start losing efficiency once they scale up to 30, 40, or above 50.

I have experienced the need to scale up teams quickly many times in my career. This means that an organization's structure must also be scalable, and this is not always done simply as a mathematical function. The components that I describe next, as well as communication and triangular leadership strategies, must guide and respond to the scaling needs of an organization. It is vital to highlight that a distributed team holds an advantage when it comes to its physical presence, after all there is no need to move to a larger building, but there is still a profound need to oversee and manage its growth to ensure its cohesiveness and balance.

The Delivery Team

A delivery team is a self-contained, empowered multi-person unit formed by members with different skill sets, and it is the presence of delivery teams that is central to developing the products that move a company toward its North Star.

The Agile methodology of software development often uses the term scrum teams. But I like delivery teams better because of its mission and its connection with the end user. Scrum teams are committed to delivering value in time-constrained slots, typically two-week sprints, whereas delivery teams leverage the continuous mindset that is constantly seeking value delivery.

A delivery team is composed of members from different disciplines and specialties that are responsible for working together to address urgent issues and the specifics of how a problem is going to be solved. Delivery teams are typically organized around product areas within products. Their members are accountable for creating the product itself from beginning to end. They don't only create the product (or parts of the product) but they also are the ones maintaining and supporting it. This sets the stage for optimized monitoring and observation, as I will describe in Chapter 7.

There also needs to be an Iron Triangle leadership dynamic in place. If a company only has delivery teams that are focused on product, for example, you have just a team of people working in isolation without input from design and engineering, that will not work. I have found this to be a common problem. People naturally try to organize delivery teams by similarities, rather than embracing the threefold dynamic of the Iron Triangle.

The Squad

Technology moves quickly. Large-scale platforms such as Facebook and Google come with their own frameworks, so if a company wants to build an app that works on both, and perhaps others, it may be necessary to adopt each of these frameworks and build for each separately. With different delivery teams working on these separate projects, it can become a nightmare for the company as a whole.

That's where the concept of the squad comes in. A squad is a group that shares the same ideals, interests, principles, and goals and possesses similar skills. It spans across delivery teams and helps facilitate collaboration and consistency. The streamlined collaboration between delivery teams mostly happens via squads, and this allows delivery teams to operate at the highest efficiency. Other large-scale software-based organizations refer to this role as a *guild*, but I have always preferred the term *squad*.

To revert to my image of the fleet of ships going to battle, imagine that *Battleship A* was preparing to go to war with an enemy that used a Google framework for its operations, while *Battleship B* was preparing to engage an enemy ship that operated on a Facebook framework. The specialist delivery teams on each battleship are working on preparing their munitions that are specific to their designated targets.

But at the same time, there are components and techniques that will be common to the teams on both battleships, such as a security protocol. The squad is the entity that can connect across ships to deliver security components or techniques that these separate delivery teams will need (Figure 6-2). Without these squads acting as connectors, the delivery teams of the respective boats must individually recreate these common security components, resulting in each boat in that fleet operating at a lower level of overall performance.

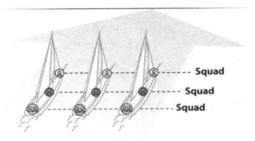

Figure 6-2. Squads

A security protocol is not a singular thing. There may be additional updates to follow, and again relying on individual delivery teams to take care of this invites trouble. Without squads, the fleet will not have a single source of truth in their security platform.

Another boating analogy to support the squad concept is weather related. In a regatta, for example, it's not right to have one boat implementing a technique for better navigation in a given type of weather while other boats flounder with the same problem. The race demands mechanisms to communicate and collaborate. It prefers the sharing of knowledge among all the boats present in the regatta and from all the boats who have sailed in earlier regattas, to ensure greater overall efficiency.

So let's take this squad analogy back on land, into the world of workplaces and teams. A company may want to establish multiple delivery teams, each guided by an Iron Triangle structure and each focusing on building a product or parts of a product. These teams, too, will benefit from the squad technique to convey and maintain the communication flow across team members ensuring the single source of truth to get work done.

It is the job of the squads to streamline the communication across to each delivery team and reinforce a collective goal. The squads don't do the actual work; the delivery teams do. The squads identify the work, collaborate across delivery teams within the same product or across products, define standards, and ensure alignment, but they don't do the work themselves. The work is brought back to the leadership of the product, formed by the Iron Triangle, and the work is prioritized accordingly.

Regardless of the motivation for its existence, each squad aims to facilitate collaboration across delivery teams, disciplines, product lines, and departments. It is helpful when squads identify and use a seamless communication channel, like a dedicated Slack channel, to keep communication clear and focused.

Squads have several specific responsibilities. They ensure that standards related to their topic are defined, documented, and followed. These standards will often be referenced in technical designs, for instance. In software development, they ensure that their squad-specific technical debt backlog is periodically groomed and maintained and that the top issues on these backlogs are identified for product and/or strategic teams to work on next.

The Two-Pizza Team

You can actually sail a 46-foot sailboat with seven people. It's possible, but not optimal. It's a big boat with a lot of moving parts and a great many things to take care of. A crew anywhere between 8 and 13 is typically better, especially for a multiday race. I have experienced all of these scenarios: I have worked on under-crewed boats and over-crewed boats. Both are problematic, even dangerous.

It's the same with delivery teams in business. You cannot have a team of one by definition. But a team of 20 might be just as bad.

To be fair to the large, global companies that I have referred to earlier, it's not like they are entirely frozen in the past. Most of them are seeking to improve and evolve, but their size—the sheer volume of their infrastructure and population—makes agility a serious challenge. They are also often global in scope with offices, campuses, and factories literally all over the globe. That's like comparing a sailboat to a supertanker, or a fleet of supertankers. You can't turn a supertanker on a dime.

But sometimes these companies have innovations that make it to the public radar. One of my favorites is Amazon's two-pizza team concept. The principle behind it is that in general, a team is ideal when it contains just the number of people required to consume two pizzas. How many should that be? Maybe eight people? This all depends on the team's mission and maybe even the size of the pizzas, and yes, there are some projects that might require a four-pizza team.

This concept should not be seen as a fixed solid line pointing to just two pizzas. It's a colorful and memorable technique for recognizing that for any committee, too many people and too few people are equally bad for its outcome. Twenty people will not get much satisfaction out of two pizzas. The number of people needed to consume two pizzas is usually a manageable one, which allows everyone to be heard. And although I have personally never, ever experienced this, imagine if no one shows up to help you eat the pizza. A one-person, two-pizza meeting will likely not end well, either.

A too-small team, or simply a team of one, not only breaks the rule of not having representation from all three sides of the Iron Triangle, but it also tends to create a hero culture where one person owns the knowledge and deliverables. That is not ideal. It is a liability to the business, and it means that the hero can't take time to think or relax because they are the only person with a hand on the tiller. That is the reason I feel delivery teams should range between five and eight people. Just like crewing a boat, there is an ideal number that is neither too few nor too many.

In this book, and in my work, I use the term "team formation" with the same intent as Amazon's two-pizza team. The goal is to determine the minimum and the maximum number of people from different specialties for each delivery team. In the same way that it is hard to sail a boat with a crew of just one or two people, it is hard to have a delivery team with just one or two people in it. The delivery team formation should always aim to maximize its own efficiency.

That means, in software development at least, the teams should be large enough to offer representation from the product management, product design, and engineering Iron Triangle plus between three and five engineers from other specialties. This may change over time depending on conditions, and the terms and titles might change for teams in other industries, but these are the types of delineators that managers should keep in mind.

Brooks's Law

When projects start running behind, it is a natural temptation for leaders to start adding more people in an attempt to catch up. Often, however, this is a counterproductive idea, and this is what famed computer architect Fred

Brooks described in his Brooks's Law, which says simply, "Adding more people to a late software project makes it later." This is because it takes time for the people added to a project to become productive, and communication overhead increases as the number of people increases.

There will always be exceptions to this rule, of course—Brooks himself acknowledges this, but overall, building a cohesive organizational structure also means you must have a team formation in place that limits the number of people that can be assigned to a delivery team.

Security Theater: Looking Behind the Curtain

A balanced team organization helps to bring efficiency to teams, but it can't happen without empowerment. Too often organizations give lip service to practices or simply embrace practices that appear to be viable, but in reality remove empowerment and productivity in the name of bland conformity. One of the best examples of this is called security theater.

Security theater is defined as implementing security measures that are "intended to provide the feeling of improved security while doing little or nothing to achieve it. Examples include tightened airport security measures or other public transport security protocols implemented after major terrorist attacks."[1] These actions look impressive but do little to fix the problem. They are typical command-and-control attempts at obfuscating problems. Security theater is a concept that many organizations suffer from but don't realize just how expensive it can be, both in terms of its cost of deployment and, worse, what gets ignored or overlooked because of it.

I faced a typical example of security theatre recently in which our IT department implemented a rule that logged everyone out from their email account after eight hours. That meant everyone had to log in again at least once or twice a day. In a world where everyone currently works from home, it is important to reflect on what this practice is trying to achieve and what better alternatives there might be. A wholesale logging-out action is destined to annoy a great many employees who will simply turn to easier and potentially less secure methods of getting their mail, sending files, or rotating easy-to-remember (and easy-to-hack) passwords.

Security theater looks like a level of security procedure is being applied, but in truth it allows more security holes to go unnoticed. For distributed teams, it's a lift and shift implementation of an already flawed approach that dilutes feelings of individual empowerment and obscures the North Star vision.

---

[1]Schneier, Bruce. (2003). *Beyond Fear: Thinking Sensibly About Security in an Uncertain World.* Copernicus Books. p. 38.

Applying These Concepts to the Distributed Team

A distributed teams approach demands a template and a leadership model that is decentralized and that empowers the people who are doing the work. Teams must have a diverse, dynamic formation; they must be neither too big nor too small, and they should align with the two-pizza concept. Team members and leaders alike should be encouraged to hold different perspectives, in order to keep the team away from the traditional command-and-control model.

Successful leadership of a distributed team, in my experience, takes into consideration all sides of the Iron Triangle. The leaders that I like to follow are those who allow me to do what I know how to do best and who are clearly able to recognize the threefold formula of people, process, and empowerment as the ingredients for success.

Key Takeaways

- Delivery teams when connected with the squad concept and the Iron Triangle completes the equation to build great products.

- The two-pizza team idea represents the vital priority of determining a team's ideal size.

- Delivery teams have the autonomy to take their own journey toward the collective North Star. The connection that delivery team members have with the end users, combined with empowerment, is what makes the approach more successful when compared to traditional agile scrum teams.

The Importance of Measurement and Metrics

All projects and teams need processes and measurements. The quote "You can't manage what you can't measure" has been used for decades in business management philosophy. It, along with variations of this quote, has been associated with W. Edwards Deming, who was one of the predominant thinkers and innovators in the fields of twentieth-century engineering and quality management.

I use this quote and I share it with the teams I lead, since measurement and metrics are vital to project management, manufacturing, and product management, and they also have a significant role to play in team management in promoting the continuous improvement mindset.

But it is equally important to recognize that measurements and metrics are only truly effective when they work in consort with effective team leadership—the human factor.

© Alberto S. Silveira Jr. 2021
A. S. Silveira Jr., *Building and Managing High-Performance Distributed Teams*,
https://doi.org/10.1007/978-1-4842-7055-4_7

Here's a quote from an article posted on the website of the W. Edwards Deming Institute that I particularly like:

> [Deming] knew that just measuring things and looking at data wasn't close to enough. There are many things that cannot be measured and still must be managed. And there are many things that cannot be measured and managers must still make decisions about.[1]

As much as metrics are vital to every project and team, being a leader and a manager means that you must consider the human aspect. Numbers, metrics, and projections are key, but many times decisions should also be taken from the human point of view.

In that same vein, leaders, especially leaders of distributed teams, should focus primarily on outcomes, rather than primarily on minutiae. As discussed earlier, trust and delegation are vital components of distributed teams management, and empowering employees to drive themselves toward their own measurable project milestones and goals is fundamental to their own motivation and sense of connection and, therefore, to the success of the project.

By contrast, when leaders stop focusing on outcomes through trust and delegation, they tend to revert to more of a top-down command-and-control mindset where micromanagement becomes the norm, which is not the way to build and run a team or to inspire high performance.

This, then, all comes full circle when we recognize that performance, by its very definition, demands measurement. Leaders might not need to measure every minute of work performed or weigh every ounce of raw material that enters the factory, but they must help establish parameters and set the goals, and this can only be done with some form of measuring device.

Measuring Speed in Knots

Measurement and metrics in any area of endeavor are vital, and this applies especially in sailing and navigation. In the centuries before radio, radar, and GPS, calculating where a vessel was vs. where it should be and also calculating how fast it was traveling were skills that relied entirely on the tools available. Speed was measured in knots and still is today.

One knot equals one nautical mile per hour, which itself is equal to 1.15 regular miles per hour. The knot-based speed measurement system was created in the 1600s and consisted simply of a rope with equally spaced knots tied along it. It was lowered into the water from the stern of a ship and had a

---

[1] https://deming.org/myth-if-you-cant-measure-it-you-cant-manage-it/

triangular-shaped wooden attachment at the far end for stability, like a plane's tailfin. The rope was played out freely for a set period of time and was then brought back on board. The number of knots that had played out in that time became the measurement of speed.

By the way, if you are wondering why a nautical mile is different from a mile on land, it's because the nautical mile is based on the most constant reference point available on the open ocean: the circumference of the Earth. Each nautical mile is equal to one minute of latitude. By contrast, the land-based mile is based on the distance that Roman soldiers could cover in one thousand paces. That's where the word comes from: the Latin for one thousand, as in *mille passus*—one thousand paces.

Project Management, Kanban, and Six Sigma

When it comes to metrics for team managers, many of the tools we now use come from the period that started at the end of the Second World War, when Europe and Japan set about building their literally shattered economies and infrastructure. These became megaprojects in which engineers from companies like General Electric, General Motors, Ford, and DuPont played a large role in developing methods for not only reconstructing industry but measuring progress and quality.

Project Management

The formalized school of project management in the United States got its start around this time, although some will debate that it started earlier, at the end of the Great Depression, with megaprojects like the construction of the Hoover Dam and America's growing network of highways and factories leading the charge.

Regardless, project management, in a nutshell, is about getting things done on time, on budget, and correctly, and I have already referred to it a couple of times in this book. It follows its own triangular relationship of *scope, time*, and *cost*, and the two words that best summarize project management success are *planning* and *communication*. Does that sound familiar? It's obviously also at the core of all successful team management.

To this day, many project managers in the United States and much of the world are trained by or follow the guidelines set by the Project Management Institute (www.pmi.org), and when I meet someone who has a Project Management Professional (PMP) designation after their name, I know they are fully capable of taking on large projects and guiding people and resources to a successful conclusion, on time, on budget, and correctly.

Kanban and DevOps

In the software development world, we have sought to combine the concepts of metrics, methods, and processes through the adoption of *kanban*, which manages workloads by "balancing demands with available capacity."

Kanban and *scrum* are the two most popular frameworks under the Agile methodology for building software teams. Distributed teams that leverage kanban use a digital board that works as a visible and tangible surface that allows team members to observe the progress of a project and actually "pull" work off the board into their laps as their time and capacity allow, rather than facing a never-ending pile of tasks being pushed at them. Kanban has been used a great deal in software development for many years now to help make decisions and prioritize work, keep team members focused, and deliver continuous value to users.

The Agile methodology, regardless of the implementation framework, focuses on making product engineering teams and development cycles more efficient and predictable. It is powerful and efficient, but it doesn't eliminate the need for having "sufficient teams." That's where DevOps comes in.

DevOps is not just a group of people that works in isolation. Rather, it represents a culture that integrates people from different specialties across multiple teams to enable continuous integration and continuous delivery.

It is a movement that helped remove the virtual walls that existed between teams allowing agile teams to be fully accountable to deliver value to users. That is the essence of the delivery team concept I mentioned in Chapter 6.

The transition from silos to integrated teams in software development took some time and practice, but it has emerged as the ideal structure for delivering reliable software applications for a high-speed marketplace.

Kanban uses cycle time as its main metric that helps team members understand the distances in time and space between point A and point B. Teams tend to increase their efficiency as they keep moving and learning from journey to journey becoming more mature as they go.

I see a direct connection between kanban and the knots on the ropes of seventeenth- and eighteenth-century sailing ships: a consistent methodology that leads to reliable measurement, which results in people knowing what to do. This creates a perfect triangular relationship of method, measurement, and people.

Six Sigma

Six Sigma, too, is a method of measurement and analysis essentially developed by Motorola as a tool for process improvement and for reducing defects.

Sigma refers to standard deviation, which in statistics refers to how a dataset is distributed relative to its mean, or average. The further away from the mean that data points are distributed, the higher the standard deviation. The number six in Six Sigma refers to the idea that it would take a "six-standard-deviation event from the mean for an error to happen. This translates to 3.4 errors out of one million events. A smaller standard deviation would mean more errors and an unacceptable level of quality."[2]

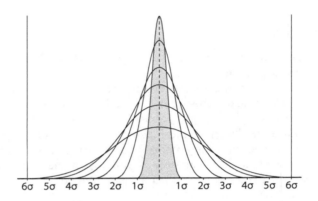

Figure 7-1. A simplified illustration of a Six Sigma curve

Figure 7-1 is a simplified representation of data deviating from the mean. But if the concept of statistics and standard deviation is not your cup of tea, don't worry. All that most of us need to remember about Six Sigma is that it seeks to establish and reduce the number of defects to a point at which output reaches 99.99966 percent perfect.

A company like Motorola or GE, which might manufacture, let's say, one million chipsets or light bulbs per day, is operating at a volume that allows them to measure defects and correlate them to manufacturing processes. By making a minute change to the parameters of their machinery, they are able to analyze increases or decreases in the number of rejected or defective parts and fine-tune their process accordingly.

This type of measurement technique is not unique to high-volume manufacturing. The concept of A/B testing follows this route and is used a great deal in Internet marketing analytics, where millions of emails or thousands of web pages can be compared and tweaked to observe the best engagement with users, even among an extremely wide range of demographics.

Amazon's online influence can be attributed, at least in part, to its highly sophisticated approach to displaying the right content to the right audience,

---

[2]Investopedia. www.investopedia.com/terms/s/six-sigma.asp, September 2020

down to the individual consumer, while using enormously powerful analytical engines to compare the success of each person's interaction with its pages.

Six Sigma is another valuable and respected professional designation, and it uses a series of colored belts to designate a student's progress, as would be seen in martial arts classes. The highest achievement is the black belt, and similar to the PMP in project management, it identifies someone who fully understands the philosophy and can teach it to others.

Other Methods

There are other metric-related techniques such as Total Quality Management (TQM), process improvement, and the variations on *kaizen*, which I will mention a few times in this book. There are detractors, of course, and some will argue that there are other, better methods of process analysis and improvement, and this is eminently possible in the era of big data, cloud computing, artificial intelligence, and machine learning. But my point is these concepts were devised and implemented to ensure that measurements and metrics were deployable and shareable, and many of them are indeed still in practice today, in just the same way that knots and miles still are. They remain reliable methods of measurement.

Alongside all the great twentieth-century luminaries and business schools, there are numerous modern thought leaders accessible today, and they too tend to highlight the need to measure what you plan to manage. *Accelerate* by Nicole Forsgren, PhD, Jez Humble, and Gene Kim is one of my favorite books at present. Written primarily for the high-pressure team environment of DevOps, the book works equally well in other industries. The authors do indeed talk about key engineering metrics, but they also emphasize the importance of building and maintaining the best team in order to create better products.

Accelerate talks about how to measure key physical metrics such as MTTR (mean time to recovery: how long it takes a machine to recover from a failure or stoppage) and deployment frequency (how long it takes teams to produce code), but it also challenges the anachronistic ideal of walls and silos as the embodiment of the workplace. They look at the need for teams to achieve milestones, but they advocate doing so by taking baby steps in the right direction: toward the collective North Star, something that goes beyond mere measurements, but is in many ways dependent on them.

Spinning Around in a Kayak

My descriptions of these methods of planning and measurement—project management, kanban, Six Sigma, TQM, and MTTR—are here because they are all techniques that are vital for effective deployment of teams and for optimized manufacture of products. They can be adapted according to the specific needs of individual market sectors, but the fact remains, without measurement tools, things become exceedingly difficult to manage consistently. They are, in a sense, the building blocks of progress.

I sail mostly on boats that require crews of between three and twelve people, but I recently worked with a client who reminded me of someone spending their first day in their new kayak. If you have ever been in a kayak, you know there's not a lot of room in there. Basically, you squeeze into this horizontal pod, and you paddle your way forward from a sitting position. There's a lot that an expert can do with a kayak including navigating dangerous rapids and currents. But until you become familiar with its unique physics, you are more likely to end up paddling in a circle. That's the state I find many companies in, which is why they call me in: to stop the spinning and start paddling in the right direction.

Why does the spinning happen? Often it's not because people aren't doing anything; it's because they are doing things—they're busy—but they are doing too much of the wrong thing, and often, they are doing this without realizing the kayak is moving in circles. Sometimes they try to use methods and metrics without budgeting the time to understand, analyze, and verify what actions are needed to course correct. For example, it's one thing to collect data, but it's something else to know what to do with it.

The Difference Between Monitoring and Observing

Collecting data enables people to observe. It's about recording numbers and facts from which you can extrapolate wisdom. Out on the water, it's the difference between looking at the sky and reading the weather. The color of the sunset or the way the wind ripples the water ahead of you may be pleasing to the passive observer, but these things are full of information to a sailor, who must be, by definition, an active observer.

Data drawn from metrics become the preliminary navigation tool that shows how to make the company or the team better through continuous improvement. But this can only happen through observation.

One great summary of the two terms, as posted in Google's Site Reliability Engineering online handbook (available at `https://landing.google.com/sre/`), describes observation as "symptom-based alerting" or in other words, to use the engineer's phrase, "what's broken and why?" The phrase "what's broken" is monitoring; asking "why" is observation.

To me, the difference between monitoring and observing is similar to the difference between knowledge and wisdom. I use it when discussing Service-Level Objectives (SLO) in the very early initial phases of building a software project, for example, to define how quickly a page should load on a website. Is two seconds acceptable? Google's current recommended page load time is under two seconds, with an ideal being half a second. If page loading currently exceeds this threshold, what should be looked at to improve? The two-second threshold represents the quality metrics of this product, while observability combined with continuous improvement and continuous testing practices lays out the path for establishing the norms required in order to meet users' expectations.

Observation Must Lead to Action and Improvement

The moral of this story is that methods, measurement, and people form another important triangular structure for building high-performance teams. There is the need to apply and constantly improve processes (in other words, application of method), there is the need to collect data and transform it into information that results in actionable improvements, and there is the need to understand, acknowledge, and work proactively with the people on the team. Similar to the Iron Triangle, all sides are required to achieve optimum outcomes.

Growth During Crisis

The last company I was with experienced substantial growth of 600 percent in terms of concurrent users using our platform, riding a crest of demand for innovation spurred by the enormous changes to commerce brought on by the pandemic. We had to keep pace, even though we were in uncharted waters.

We grew as a company because the demand for our services increased exponentially overnight. This might be every entrepreneur's dream, but unmanageable growth can be just as fatal to a company as product failure or getting overtaken by a goliath competitor.

We followed a streamlined communication and growth plan to counter the turbulence of this rapid expansion. We used guidelines and processes to ensure every team member knew what to do, and we stuck to them. During times of crisis or growth, leaders and team members might identify a process that could be improved. But in my experience at least, I feel such discoveries should wait until after we have crossed the finish line and emerged from the current crisis. That's what the race is about. As I will describe in Chapter 15, switching plans in the middle of a race can have unwelcome consequences.

You can still strike a balance between principles of continuous improvement on the one hand and the careful adherence to the existing plan on the other, by ensuring team members are able and encouraged to take notes and communicate their ideas, recording them in a central knowledge base for review and deployment later. It is during periods of action that empowered people do their best critical thinking. When they are focused on their task at hand, without undue stress or pressure, guided by well-planned and practiced guidelines and processes, they are simultaneously best positioned for those "what if" or "aha" moments. They should be allowed to pause long enough to take some improvement notes, for later review by the team.

This is where your communication culture, process, and North Star come in to play—reinforcing concentration and innovation while doing what we know how to do best.

I will discuss knowledge bases in Chapter 8 and continuous improvement in Chapter 12.

Guidelines and Processes in a Rescue Situation

If you are out on the water in a sailboat and there are no other boats nearby and someone from your boat falls into the water, how do you stop in order to perform the rescue? A sailboat doesn't have brakes, and you can't throw it into reverse and back up. Stopping a boat is an exercise in physics, guided by practice and a cool mind.

You must bring the boat around in a big circle, aiming to get as close to the person as possible. The circle maneuver converts most of the forward momentum into centrifugal force, which will slow the boat down and bring it to a near stop as close to the person as possible. You only have one chance at this.

Bringing the boat to a near stop is vital here because it is extremely dangerous to try to grab a person and lift them out of the water while a boat is in motion, even slow motion. A person in the water will now present a mass of twice or more of their regular weight, which will simply succeed in pulling the rescuer overboard.

In an overboard scenario, there also needs to be a watcher. The person who sees someone fall overboard must never take their eyes off the victim. Ever. Not until rescue has been completed. They must point at the victim and just keep pointing and keep staring. This is because out on the water, it is easy to lose track of something as small as a person's head amid the waves.

Now hopefully these three scenarios, the circle, the lift, and the watcher, help to illustrate the importance of practiced scenarios in times of crisis or unexpected change. People need to learn and practice their roles. They need to understand and adhere to procedures, and they need to overrule their own instincts for spontaneous action. The time for review and retrospective will come later.

Observability and Metrics During the 2020 Pandemic

Sustainability and growth aren't possible without observability, and this goes double during a major world crisis, like the 2020 pandemic. The company I was working with during this time delivered online learning solutions, the demand for which exploded exponentially as people of all ages were forced to do their learning from home.

We had to measure everything to make sure the systems were responding and operating as required to handle an unprecedented load. Any unusual patterns in utilization would not be noticeable without a close comparison of historical and real-time metrics. Without this information, it would not have been possible for our teams and technology to respond in time to ensure the applications remained available and reliable to millions of concurrent users.

We wouldn't have been able to ride this tsunami of demand if we had not established metrics and a culture of observability and then taught these concepts to our teams.

Redefining Urgency

Urgency is a term that I like to use to describe positive energy. Some may think of the word in relation to a dangerous or bad situation, like a deadline with negative repercussions. But I like to use the word urgency as something that conveys energy and passion. Perhaps that's because English is my second language.

When you learn a new language, you cannot help but want to examine every word: What does it mean? Why do people choose to use this particular word over a different one? Your mother tongue gets absorbed into yourself as part of the growing process. It comes from immersion and the enviable capacity kids have to basically slurp up everything they see around them and store it in their hungry brains. But when you have to learn something consciously and methodically, you get more of a chance to vet it first, which, again I hope you can see, applies not only to learning language but also to learning procedure.

So, to me, urgency is the urge to move forward, to achieve, to progress. Welcoming urgency into your life is a great way to avoid destructive habits and wasteful conditions such as procrastination. It's the discovery of the positive emotional energy that is tied to your team's efforts and is guided by your North Star.

A team's sense of urgency happens when team members connect to the North Star.

Urgency is not about micromanaging. It's not about counting the hours worked by your team members. It's about outcomes.

High-performance teams do not run on conveyor belts or hamster wheels. Their sense of urgency does not come from a threat of punishment. It comes from ensuring that every individual is connected to the North Star, goals, and mission. It goes back to bringing in people that align with your passion as a leader.

The companies that get this, even if they don't understand all the ins and outs of it, possess the wherewithal to thrive and grow, even in the face of much larger competitors.

As a leader in this space, I know that. If our organization is symbolized once again as a boat, without my passion, my urgency, and my ability to align the passions of my distributed team to our North Star, the boat won't just simply sit motionless in the water—it will sink.

Think of urgency as practiced readiness. Or measured readiness. Whichever works for you.

Key Takeaways

- Measurement techniques apply to procedures as much as they do to physical items. Concepts like Six Sigma and project management are established and proven measurement techniques.

- Many organizations may be aware of measurement techniques but have not yet learned how to use them properly.

- Monitoring of activities must lead to observation, which together point the way toward excellence and ongoing improvement.

Streamlining the Collaboration Process

There comes a time in the life of every company or team where things either start to fly apart or at least threaten to. Keeping a team together and riding through this particular type of storm is dependent in great measure on the abilities of the leader to anticipate such challenges, identify the best route forward, and use data and metrics as a guide.

For example, within a company that creates something, whether it's a physical product like a widget or lines of code in software development or a service, things can start to fly apart due to an increase in demand, changes to a production schedule, or perhaps a massive failure or disruption, of which the 2020 pandemic must rate as one of the largest.

Changes or disruptions might also be cultural. In my world of software development, the pace of change has demanded that technicians who used to work on either side of a metaphorical wall, primarily code writers and code testers, are now working closer together—so close, in fact, that their responsibilities are blending. This has caused significant disruption.

© Alberto S. Silveira Jr. 2021
A. S. Silveira Jr., *Building and Managing High-Performance Distributed Teams*,
https://doi.org/10.1007/978-1-4842-7055-4_8

Distributed teams face similar challenges. As much as it might appear wonderful at first glance for knowledge workers to get to work from anywhere, there are reasons why, up until this period in history, people were expected to arrive at a place of work. The workplace was built as a focal space where work could happen. It was often far from perfect, but it was designed for the activities of business to take place.

It is a mistake for companies to try to "lift and shift" the habits and processes of a workplace and position them directly on top of the members of a distributed team. Regardless of whether these distributed team members work from home offices or commercial satellite offices, there is already a strong need to streamline the process to match their context.

The habits of the traditional office cannot be applied to distributed teams.

Streamlining: The Triangle of the Three Ms

One of the most significant developments that came from the use of project management, Six Sigma, and the other techniques I described in Chapter 7 is the Toyota Production Management (TPM) process that was so instrumental to productivity and streamlining in heavy industry. One of the many great concepts from TPM is the triangle of *Muda, Mura,* and *Muri.* These are Japanese terms that describe wastefulness, unevenness, and unreasonable overburden in the manufacturing process, and over the decades, they became fundamental to the Lean Process Management school. In essence, the three Ms help reinforce a streamlined process by removing the parts that are bulky, redundant, or just plain wasteful.

This is yet another concept that is no longer exclusive to manufacturing. Let's look at it in the context of team communication. Email and messaging apps like Slack or Microsoft Teams can be excellent tools, but without guidance, they too can gum up the works, usually by expanding beyond a manageable size. For email, this might mean having a culture of too many emails. For messaging apps, this might mean having too many channels resulting in people talking about the same topic in different places.

My point is that people are being bombarded with messages and notifications every day all day long with emails, chat messages, video calls, and even traditional direct phone calls and SMSs. The opposite of streamlined communication is chaos. When we expect people to manage a variety of communication channels, confusion and time wastage become the norm.

The opposite of streamlined communication is chaos.

Streamlining is not just about opening a new channel on your new internal collaboration app. It's about establishing and following guidelines for synchronous and asynchronous communication that use as few channels as possible and which respect people's time.

When you have streamlined communication guidelines where teams have predefined agreements on how to interact, the number of channels that can be managed by people can be brought back down to a collection that is economical, clear, and practical. People will know where to go to find what they need when they need it. Techniques like using something as simple as a prefix or suffix for naming convention in chat applications or emails allow people to avoid the wastefulness, unevenness, and unreasonable overburden of the three Ms and improve team communication and comprehension.

Streamlining Communication: The Origins of Seaspeak

Boats and planes use numerous techniques to streamline collaboration and ensure safety. One that almost everyone has heard of is the NATO phonetic alphabet, otherwise known as the ICAO (International Civil Aviation Organization) alphabet, in which each letter is given a word to represent it, such as Alpha, Bravo, Charlie, Delta, Echo, and so on. This is done to ensure that letters and numbers are not misunderstood when spoken over radio communications, which are often full of static. Think, for example, how similar the letters "S" and "F" sound to each other as well as to the word "yes."

The NATO phonetic alphabet is just one of many streamlined processes that have been adapted worldwide to increase efficiency and safety. Another is the adoption of the English language as the official universal language of communication for pilots all over the world. This, again, is to ensure safety and consistency. For example, even if a civilian aircraft (cargo or passenger) belonging to a non-English-speaking nation is flying within its own borders, there remains a risk that it might encounter another plane or be forced to divert to an airport elsewhere. To ensure clarity in any situation, all pilots must be proficient in English to a standard set by the ICAO.

The same used to be true for shipping, but in recent years, the proportion of native English speakers within shipping crews has substantially upended to the degree that now, 80 percent do not speak English. To avoid miscommunication and to improve efficiency of ship operation, there is a new, streamlined method of onboard communication called Seaspeak, which is now recognized as the official language of the seas by the International Maritime Organization.

Seaspeak still uses English as its base, but it has specific rules on how to talk on a ship's radio, including limiting the number of words in a message and requiring that each message starts with a *message marker* that tells the crew what type of message is upcoming. There are eight message markers currently in operation. They are Advice, Answer, Information, Instruction, Intention, Question, Request, and Warning. In addition, double-digit numbers, like 42, are spoken as "four-two," and clock times are also spoken as words and always refer to Coordinated Universal Time, which is the time currently at zero degrees longitude and is never adjusted for daylight saving time.

Streamlining Processes Does Not Always Mean Minimizing Them

Often, when someone thinks of streamlining in terms of design, they picture something with smooth, sharp lines like a jet fighter or a speedboat. These certainly do cut down on certain types of wind or water resistance, but there are also other ways to increase efficiency.

For example, many civilian airliners now employ "winglets," which are wingtip extensions bent by 90 degrees. Depending on the size of the plane, these winglets can be up to eight feet tall. Despite their size and non-streamlined appearance, they have been proven to reduce drag and provide extra lift.

Similarly, if you have ever seen an ocean-going freighter riding high in the water after having been unloaded, you will likely see a bulbous extension on the bow (Figure 8-1). This device, which usually sits below the waterline, helps break up the mass of seawater or ice, allowing both to flow past the hull with less resistance.

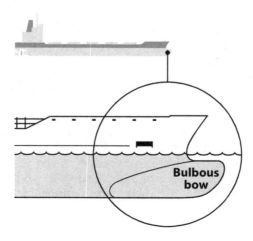

Figure 8-1. Bulbous extension

So, in both cases, these are non-streamlined extensions that serve to improve the motion of planes and ships, by relating to the context of their situation. This shows that air and water resistance can be defeated by more than just smooth lines.

Streamlining is vital to effective team management and is dependent on the interpretation of metrics. Methods that improve processes might come from removing wasteful tasks or adding or changing tasks that improve the efficiency of a process. I think of it as a technique that provides access to a single, searchable source of truth for policies, guidelines, and standards, accessible to everyone and understandable by everyone. And by accessible I mean not only readable but also something that people feel empowered to edit and improve at any time. That is the opposite of minimizing.

Case Study: We Need More Memory

I once experienced a perfect opportunity for streamlining with a company I was working with. I had a group of software engineers that, to complete their work, needed a computer system with 32 gigs of memory, even though the "standard issue" was 16 gigs. For two weeks, my managers and I had to run back and forth between departments to find a way to get my people 32 gigs. The standard response received was "That's not in the budget."

This was a company that still considered itself to be in that young aggressive mindset, but had already moved across to a stratum of management that sought to pull back on expenses that it independently deemed as excessive. A physical product order that might have amounted to an extra cost of $400 per machine became mired in discussions and handoffs from department to department, manager to manager, wasting time—mine, the managers', and the engineers'—that for sure amounted to much more than the initial additional $400.

At the end of the day, the lack of streamlining between IT's goals and engineering's goals meant

- Expenses were incurred in handling the back-and-forth between IT and engineering that far exceeded the cost of buying the additional 16 GB memory for the computers.

- There was a negative impact on customers who had to wait longer to get the features they wanted.

- Frustration grew within departments due to the nondelivery of the much-needed 32 GB computers and due also to the stubborn insistence from IT to stay on budget despite the fiscal advantages the upgrade would have delivered.

This lack of cross-departmental alignment may look like a simple bureaucratic disagreement, but it does great damage to a team's efforts to align with its North Star. It was an example of the old English idiom of being "penny wise and pound foolish."

The Three Strategies for Streamlined Communication

Streamlining collaboration relies on having a communication process that serves as a single, searchable source of truth for guidelines, policies, and standards and which is equally accessible to in-person and distributed team members. This is intended to be a living, breathing document, meaning individuals are empowered to improve its sections to maximize ownership and buy-in while ensuring consistency and alignment through effective governance. You will notice once again how there is a triangular relationship concept going on here: three key items that together help to establish a high-performance culture while maintaining stability.

Strategy No. 1: Documentation

Teams should be given access to a centralized knowledge base solution where all documentation lives. This knowledge base should be permanently accessible to everybody, with established guidelines for how and what to document, common definitions and terms, and a constantly updated record of changes available to everyone. A documentation strategy needs active knowledge management, so that its pages do not become a write-only memory. It is important to define the mechanisms for maintaining and disseminating these contents. The Wiki model works well for this (see Chapter 14).

One of the key elements of a documentation strategy will be a glossary of essential terms and definitions that are to be used. For example, I place a great deal of importance around clear definitions and usage of processes, procedures, standards, and policies, all of which tend to get used interchangeably, but shouldn't (my definitions of each are listed in Chapter 12). Similarly, there will be a need for industry-specific searchable terms as well as culturally appropriate terminologies, especially when referring to people. The glossary should be a go-to place for ensuring people are speaking the same, correct language.

Strategy No. 2: Communication

It is vital to establish an agreed-upon set of tools with defined use cases and expectations that reduce calendar fragmentation, increase productivity, improve work relationships, provide clarity and agreement on how to communicate, accommodate diversity, create synergy, and reduce the need for expensive synchronous meetings. These can include such simple processes as agreeing upon communication channels, calendar invite and video chat meeting link protocol, as well as the acceptance and use of practices like Focus Time (described later in this chapter).

Strategy No. 3: Meetings

Develop or adopt a process to ensure the effectiveness of meetings, which includes creating and distributing a clear agenda in advance, using follow-up action items, surveys, capturing important takeaways and making them available to everyone, using collaboration tools that everyone can access, making full use of video chat technology, maximizing engagement, and overall ensuring everyone's time is used productively.

The strategies described are all commonsense items, but the passage of time, along with people's natural tendency to revert to older, less effective habits, means that proactive continuous improvement steps must be made. These include placing these ideas and objectives into a formalized document as a means of furthering comprehension and buy-in, as well as regularly scheduling follow-ups and refreshers to ensure the habits become a permanent part of the culture.

Going Synchronous or Asynchronous

One of the best ways a distributed team can launch and maintain a culture of efficiency and continuous improvement is through its choice of synchronous and asynchronous communication techniques. Communication is obviously fundamental to a team's ongoing success, whether that team is widely distributed or working together in the same physical office space. The key is ensuring everyone knows how to use it.

The terms *synchronous* and *asynchronous* should be self-explanatory in terms of how they work: Synchronous communication happens in real time. This includes in-person meetings, phone conversations, video chats, and face-to-face communication. Asynchronous communication happens outside of real time. The most obvious and oldest example of this would be writing a letter or sending an email, in which one person prepares and sends a message, which is then transported to someone else who will read it.

Text messaging via SMS or through an online chat platform like Slack, Signal, or WhatsApp could be seen as either synchronous or asynchronous, depending on how the participants decide to interact—immediately or later.

For most of history, the only way for people to be able to have a synchronous meeting was for them to all be together in the same room. Churches, temples, schools, castle courtyards—these were the spaces that were available for a group of people to hear the same message at the same time. That's where the term *audience* comes from after all—a group of people being able to *hear* the same thing at the same time.

But this, obviously, is no longer the case. But because in-person, same-place meetings have been a staple of work life for everyone, they still seem to be the obvious go-to whenever there is a need to share information in real time. But this needs to change.

The Hidden Cost of Synchronous Meetings

The most common example of multi-person synchronous communication in the work environment is the meeting. In theory, a meeting is an ideal method of distributing knowledge and sharing creativity among a group of people. But in practice, meetings have become expensive and time-consuming activities that are the source of much time wastage and disillusionment and seldom deliver the value in terms of person-minutes invested.

This is not because a meeting is a necessarily impractical activity, at least in theory; it's just that people, over time, tend to revert to bad or wasteful habits. This, by the way, is why the *kaizen* concept of continuous improvement is so vital to high-performance distributed teams and why I will refer to it a few more times in this book.

When you have people sitting around a boardroom table or on a video chat, the meter is always running. Each of these people has an hourly fee. If you have a panel of lawyers billing out at $600 per hour, you will likely be painfully aware of the mounting cost. Time, after all, is money. The same applies if you have other consultants or subcontractors. They often bill by the hour, regardless of what is happening.

This hourly billing concept is something that everyone should keep in mind. It's an excellent way to remember the value of time, even among those who do not formally bill by the hour. Salaried employees, too, have an hourly rate, even though it's not always obvious. Your people might work for a five-figure or six-figure annual salary, but in truth, it still comes down to an hourly rate.

These people around your meeting room table or on your video chat screen, then, are each charging you and your company for an hour of their time spent in this meeting space, regardless of whether there is some vibrant progress being made in the meeting or if everyone is making small talk as they wait for latecomers to arrive.

If you want another real-world example, think about what it is like to sit in the back of a taxi, while stuck in traffic. Prior to services like Uber and Lyft, taxis were the main way to get around town, and no matter whether you were moving or stopped, the meter kept running. That, by the way, is where the word taxi came from in the first place—it's based on the French term for tariff meter, which they called a *taximetre*.

When it comes to the money that a company pays for its own people to attend the meeting, I always feel the true cost should be doubled to factor not only the time an employee is spending in the meeting but also the value of what else they could have been doing with their time at that moment. Every time the meeting facilitator says, "We are missing two people who are not here yet, so let's give them a few minutes, then we'll get started," this wastes money, time, and talent.

There is even software available that can calculate the cost of a meeting for you. Whether you use such software or not, it becomes easy to understand why meetings are consistently identified as the number one time-waster in all of business. They tend to be run too casually and without an awareness of the per-minute cost vs. intended ROI.

I recognize that in my preceding example of meetings that start late because "we are missing two people," those in attendance can salvage the time by taking care of emails or other work on their laptops, and I recognize too that taxis sometimes used a reduced fare for traffic jams and other congestion— but not always. Regardless, such concessions fail to make up for a well-planned and timely event. The hourly rate of salaried employees should always be seen as an investment that yields dividends rather than a sunk cost. A manager's awareness of invisible elements such as an employee's de facto hourly rate should be as tangible as a ticking *taximetre*.

But look at what happened in 2020. To preserve the imperfect meeting culture of the on-premises office in a period of lockdown, the whole thing was lifted and shifted into the video chat environment. Teams were expected to continue doing the same type of work in the same way as they had been doing back at the office, using video chat to replace the meeting room, and the results were not exciting.

I have spoken with managers who have expressed how fatigued they and their team members have become after attending uncountable hours of video chat meetings. I have also seen organizations that for years had scheduled professional development or training days for staff and that thought that the same eight-hour workshop could be delivered in an eight-hour live video session. That decision did not go well, either.

People believe that synchronous communication automatically moves things forward. That's not true. It's not automatic. Video chat technology has tremendous potential as the new standard of collaboration, but deploying it by using only a *lift* and *shift* method tends to reinforce the worst parts of an existing culture rather than building a new, better one. Team members are left with a growing awareness of micromanagement and an implicit lack of trust at a time when these new tools should be delivering optimism, enthusiasm, and tangible performance improvement.

How to Streamline the Collaboration Process

The transition into a mature collaboration process for distributed teams will take a little time, planning, and practice. The building blocks are already in place: video, sound, and interactive online collaboration tools all deliverable by high-bandwidth Internet. The challenge now is how to make this a new language and culture in and of its own, just like Seaspeak.

Part of this will depend on learning new physical skills such as talking, listening, and working together in a virtual environment—this includes small but important human actions like making eye contact on screen—as well as more streamlined logistics, such as scheduling and sending meeting links and calendar appointments. These might all seem like incredibly small and pedestrian details, but they have great impact on the success of a virtual meeting. A great deal of frustration can be avoided simply by ensuring everyone on a distributed team is comfortable with video chat technology, has it reliably and securely installed, and has a link to the meeting and a calendar invite (see Strategy No. 2 of section "The Three Strategies for Streamlined Communication" earlier in this chapter).

On a slightly larger scale, you could summarize streamlined collaboration as "knowing where to go to find the people or the knowledge you need," whether this is a person with the right amount of authority or skill or information that is easily findable, like a centralized knowledge base (see Strategy No. 1 earlier).

Workflow: The Benefits of Streamlined Time

Whether the members of a distributed team are located within a single time zone or not, there should still be a system by which time itself is coordinated to ensure smooth workflow between all the components of a productive day.

Many books have spoken about successful time management practices in the workplace. Two of my favorites are *Cool Time: A Hands-On Plan for Managing Work and Balancing Time* by Steve Prentice and *Remote: Office Not Required* by Jason Fried and David Heinemeier Hansson. Both of these books stress the importance of dividing the day up to correctly handle the three most vital components of work: (1) periods of undisturbed self-directed work, which I and the authors refer to as Focus Time, (2) mutually convenient time slots for Collaboration Time, and (3) time for catching up with emails and project planning of tasks and work inventory.

Many people struggle with time and tasks because they mix these three concepts up each day, trying to do parts of each of these without any structure or sequence. When that happens in manufacturing, the results are a mess, which is why project management, Six Sigma, and TQM and others all came about: you need a process to get things done correctly.

In project management, this means traveling along a sequential five-step process (Initiation, Planning, Execution, Control, and Closure). In manufacturing, it will be based on one or more processes to ensure that, in essence, raw materials pass through a factory in one direction one time—in one door and out another while meeting quality standards and seeking continuous improvement at all times. In the development of software products, the left-to-right concept is similar, although it has been refined substantially since the days of Waterfall. (Waterfall is another concept from the software development industry, in which a product moves in steps from phase to phase. As I will describe in greater detail in Chapter 14, this has been substantially improved upon in recent years.)

For the sometimes unstructured work of a day in an office, there is equal opportunity for organization and streamlining. That's what time management is all about: segmenting Focus Time, Collaboration Time, and Catch-up Time in a way that works for everyone.

Focus Time

Quite simply, the concept of Focus Time is a block of time—let's say an hour—in which a person focuses on the task at hand, does not respond to emails or other types of messaging, does not receive visitors (in person or virtual), and does not join meetings or video chats.

The benefits of undisturbed time come not just from the lack of interruptions, but that quite simply, your brain can do better when it feels good about its situation, and this is done by (1) booking off Focus Time in your calendar, (2) ensuring your team members accept and respect this time, and (3) giving team members tangible awareness as to when the Focus Time will be over.

Blocking off Focus Time allows you to work without a sense of guilt or preoccupation, but instead with a fully fueled, fully focused creative mind. Giving people awareness as to when it will end makes it much easier for them to accept it and work their priorities around it.

One of the metrics I like to pay close attention to is the amount of Focus Time my engineers get on a weekly basis. When I observe that it is trending to less than 55–60 percent of their time on average, I take action in several ways:

- I speak directly to their managers to ensure they increase the amount of Focus Time available to the individual engineers.

- I revisit and analyze the effectiveness of meetings being held, to see whether there are too many of them and whether any can be combined, canceled, or replaced by other techniques such as asynchronous communication.

- I work to identify ways for team members to implement Focus Time in a way that works for the whole team. One simple example of this is to allow Focus Time to occur during mornings, while meetings can only happen in afternoons. Not everyone schedules Focus Time for exactly the same hour, but this binary approach substantially cuts down on meetings being jeopardized by Focus Time and vice versa.

All in all, I do these because Focus Time is one of the most important contributing factors to high-performance distributed teams, since it gives people the time and space to do what they know how to do best.

Collaboration Time

Applying the Focus Time model described earlier to a distributed team is far easier when everyone works in a similar time zone, as I have already mentioned. The challenge is always around how to balance Focus Time with time for collaboration, not only with team members within the same time zone but also for those whose days are a couple of hours ahead or behind your own.

This is part of what streamlining and evolving an entirely new approach to work is all about. Adjacent time zones are not barriers to distributed teams' productivity. They are delineation points that provide windows for communication while maintaining realistic opportunities for Focus Time to occur. Team members can use shared calendars, for instance, to identify times where communication can happen, as well as when they shouldn't. It is not difficult to set up guidelines for both, especially when availabilities and non-availabilities are accessible to everyone in the team.

People who work in the Eastern time zone, on the eastern side of the United States, and who have clients or team members on the west coast, can strategically enjoy three hours of "quiet time" before their west coast colleagues get started. Similarly, west coasters get some quiet time around 2:00 PT when their east coast colleagues sign off. This is a generalization, of course. Not everyone gets to maintain strict nine-to-five hours—that too is a holdout from a previous era, but nonetheless, there are distinct patterns of availability that are inescapably influenced by time zones, and these should be addressed and leveraged.

This is where the skills of modern time management and team management really come into play. It's not that difficult to coordinate Focus Time and Collaboration Time, using both synchronous and asynchronous communication tools. It's not that difficult at all, but it does require planning, as we will see in more detail in the following.

That's why the term "time management" has two words in it. The second word is "management." Contrary to the assumptions that some people hold, the word "management" does not in fact refer to "managing to survive," but is instead pointing to the proactive management of time and tasks, using those two techniques I mentioned earlier as being central to the success of any project: planning and communication.

Proactive management of schedules means you can manage schedules so that teams can decrease their calendars' fragmentation, thus maximizing the balance between Collaboration Time and Focus Time.

A couple of centuries ago, asynchronous communication was all we had. You would have to handwrite a letter, longhand, using quill pen and ink, and then give it to someone who would give it to someone else on horseback, and in the case of international correspondence, there was the weeks or months that your letter would sit in the hold of a ship, before being given to people on horseback or on foot at the other end. We have replaced all of that with superhigh-speed Internet communication, reducing the time a message needs to travel across the world from months to seconds. Surely we can use a little of that time saved to invest in proactive management?

By contrast, when people are not allowed to work undisturbed, we get a domino effect of chaos in which people all work in a state of distraction and disorientation. That's why company presidents have offices with doors and usually a gatekeeper/executive assistant posted outside. Senior company officials have learned that their time is valuable and that it must be defended.

I suggest that all members of a team should feel the same about their own work, and even though they may not wield the authority to close their door or close themselves off in the same way the executives can, with a little explanation and proactive teaching to your team members, this balance between Focus Time and Collaboration Time will work.

Catch-up Time

Catch-up Time is time reserved for the vital maintenance work of the day. Whereas Focus Time is for self-directed work on a top-priority task and Collaboration Time is for working together with other team members, it is vital to also ensure time is reserved for looking after the maintenance tasks, so that they do not get backlogged and so that nothing is missed. Maintenance includes lower-priority tasks such as catching up on emails and messages, but it is also about taking care of secondary activities that do not need team collaboration. Of vital importance here is that Focus Time is reserved ideally for the time of day when you are at your mental and physiological best, allowing you to apply the best of yourself to the most important tasks. Tasks such as email should be assigned to those times in the day when your energy is not at its peak.

A one-on-one meeting could be considered a catch-up activity even though it leverages synchronous communication between two people especially if it is an opportunity to learn from each other rather than working on a top-priority task. It is relatively easy for two people to accommodate time to catch up. An easy way to distinguish a catch-up activity that involves another person from a collaboration event is that collaboration focuses on the team while catch-up focuses on the individual.

Scheduling catch-up items into a day is as vital to the success of projects as cleaning decks and hulls is to the maintenance of a boat. It might look like tedious custodial work, but it clears a path for high performance. This is not a new concept. Most books on productivity and excellence will refer to the importance of reserving time for these types of support or logistical activities, because without them, the higher-priority activities will inevitably suffer.

Allotments of time in this fashion can pose a challenge to action-oriented people, especially Type A personalities, for whom the apparent custodial quality of catch-up activities does not sync with their internal drive. By calling it Catch-up Time, we give it a brand, a mnemonic that helps make it real, which in turn helps legitimize its place on the calendar, especially for people whose impulsive personalities might dismiss such things or simply forget to do them.

How much time should be reserved for Catch-up Time? That can best be determined by looking at the amount of custodial work a person does in a day. Email tends to arrive in an ad hoc fashion throughout the day, but if you were to stop and add up the amount of time in total that was spent daily on emails (writing them as well as reading them), it would become possible to essentially take inventory of this task and budget for it accordingly.

If you deduce that you need to spend two hours a day on emails, this first gives you a chance to practice the streamlining concepts described earlier, especially the *wastefulness sections within the TPM concepts* of Muda, Mura, and Muri. Second, if two hours for email is determined to be appropriate and useful, then this allows you to budget two hours per day, solely for the catch-up activity of dealing with email.

Maybe you will divide these two hours into three 40-minute segments over the course of each day, but the point remains: you translate that email inventory into Catch-up Time so that you can maintain the backlog while still responding to messages in a timely fashion.

Last but not least, it's important to once again reference latitude and longitude into this equation. Time zones are important for scheduling Catch-up Time. When team members are 12 hours apart, one-on-one discussions can be a challenge.

The Power of Three: Focus, Collaboration, and Catch-up

Figure 8-2 illustrates just how well the triangle of Focus Time, Collaboration Time, and Catch-up Time can apply across the adjacent time zones of a distributed team, increasing individual and team productivity through transparency of communication.

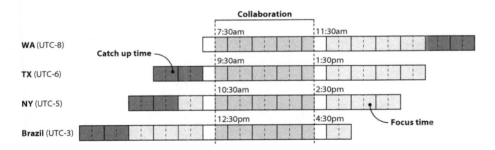

Figure 8-2. Time alignment mapping

The ideal *hot zone* for collaboration occurs where all the adjacent time zones reflect commonly convenient time that occurs during daylight, in this case, 7:30–11:30 a.m. Pacific Time. Adjacent to this hot zone is Catch-up Time for emails and planning and proactive expectation management (informing people about your plans), as well as Focus Time.

Imagine how much easier this is for team members when they can all see this same calendar at the same time, on their screens, and be able to work at times where natural light helps boost energy, attention, and performance. This is an example of living the expression of all being on the same page. It becomes much easier for people to work to a schedule like this when they can actually see it.

Key Takeaways

- Streamlining practices is a vital part of an effective team environment, which is why techniques such as the ICAO alphabet and Seaspeak came into existence.

- Streamlining also applies to the events of the day, including meetings, collaboration, and self-directed work.

- A day that includes time for focus, collaboration, and catch-up is ideally structured for optimum productivity for individuals and teams alike.

Empowering Team Members to Seek the North Star

Building and managing a successful distributed team requires more than communication technology and time management skills. This is also about dealing with a group of people who are physically separate from each other and who need to coexist socially and emotionally. They need to be aware of their company's North Star as individuals and as a community, and they need to be empowered and feel motivated to constantly follow and contribute to it. The mechanical aspects described in the previous chapter go a long way toward making this possible, of course, but I feel that *streamlined collaboration* goes at least one step further than this. Streamlined collaboration means making life easier. It establishes and reinforces the process for people to

© Alberto S. Silveira Jr. 2021
A. S. Silveira Jr., *Building and Managing High-Performance Distributed Teams*,
https://doi.org/10.1007/978-1-4842-7055-4_9

communicate most effectively, so that they genuinely feel part of a community. Remote means being cut off from the main social body; distributed means the social body is the collective of all the distanced members.

Remote means being cut off from the main social body. Distributed means the social body is the collective of all the distanced members.

The Power of Empowerment: Toyota, Amazon, and...the NYC Subway?

One of the best ways to support a culture of collectivity in any team, but especially a distributed team, is to ensure there is a tangible and well-used currency of empowerment. So to see how that works, let's take a trip on my city's subway system.

The New York City Subway system is one of the most intricate and well-established transportation systems in the world. It started operations in 1904, and by 2019, it was transporting 5.5 million riders every weekday. It is owned by the city of New York who leases it to the New York City Transit Authority, a subsidiary of the state-run Metropolitan Transportation Authority (MTA). The city and the transit authorities work hard to make sure that the people who ride the system feel that they are part of its community, by encouraging them to share the responsibility for its overall safety. This is best embodied by its security tagline: *if you see something, say something.*

The subway system is not the only organization to have used this message, of course, but it fits the bill in terms of distributing the responsibility of mutual safety among all its riders. Think about how different it would feel if, instead, the security tagline read: *we're looking out for you.* This might be a comforting sentiment, but it is not empowering. It would move the responsibility of safety back to the Metropolitan Transport Authority alone where it would live inside a command-and-control silo.

By sharing the responsibility and by reinforcing the sense of the common good that can come from this tagline, the subway's management structure is delivering a sense of empowerment to its ridership.

Empowerment means giving the choice and authority for individuals to act, without waiting for clearance from higher-ups and without fear of repercussion. To build a culture of empowerment, an organization must clearly define its goals and expectations, create the environment for individuals to embrace the cause, allow for failure, celebrate victories, and repeat the message, the education, and the reinforcement regularly.

Empowerment represents autonomy, but it's an autonomy that supports the organization and the common good. When people feel empowered, they recognize that each task they embrace is paired with a sense of responsibility and connectedness to their team. Empowerment demands a tangible demonstration of trust from an employer or manager and must be repaid in kind through responsible and thoughtful independent actions on the part of the individual.

In the case of the New York City Subway system, the policy of *if you see something, say something* represents an empowerment bestowed upon every rider and employee. The end benefit is increased security, but its side benefits include (hopefully) a more responsible use of the transit system by people who feel in some small way a co-ownership of its success and status.

The empowering statement *if you see something, say something* applies equally well to any organization interested in continuous improvement. It lives at the heart of the process called *kaizen*, most famously applied to the Toyota Production System (TPS) in Japan. TPS empowered employees to take action if they identified a fault or defect on their production lines. They were required to pull on a cord—a physical rope called an Andon cord—to stop production on an assembly line if a defect was visible. The manager would then visit the worker and issue thanks for pulling the cord. This was known as the *gemba* walk. The team would then work together to fix the problem, recognizing that by doing things in this order, much larger delays were being avoided.

Amazon, unquestionably a world leader in a wide range of business, commerce, and technology practices, prioritizes the customer experience over almost every other aspect of their business, and they use an Andon cord to help them achieve their customer satisfaction goals. When a customer calls Amazon customer service to report a problem or defect in a product, the representative is empowered to "pull the cord," completely removing the product from distribution until the problem has been fixed. This process has prevented an enormous amount of larger customer service issues for Amazon.[1]

Just like Six Sigma discussed earlier, there are some organizations and thinkers who suggest such concepts like the Andon cord may have run their course, but I feel that the quest for continuous improvement can never go out of style, and when organizations like Amazon embrace it, you can be sure they know what they are doing.

When every person in the team is empowered to see something, say something, and do something, it does not need to be solely about security. It is about giving team members the individual responsibility to observe and act in the interest of the team's collective advancement. The success of a team

---

[1] Retrieved from Six Sigma Daily. www.sixsigmadaily.com/what-is-an-andon-cord/

then becomes the success of each individual. For distributed teams, communalizing the responsibility through a social media–style model will actually make it easier to improve and further streamline the collective work process.

Team Alignment Is Key: Across Departments Too

Guidelines and shared knowledge help create a smooth flow of ideas across teams and departments. Empowerment reduces procedural bottlenecks. Trust encourages self-sufficiency and responsible behavior. These concepts are as vital to the cohesiveness of distributed teams as they are for on-premises. Communication and documentation strategies increase the productivity of teams. They provide clarity to people and alignment to the North Star. They respect diversity, allowing people to work on their schedule more efficiently. Communication and documentation strategies also increase the efficiency of the decision-making process, and last but not least, they inject transparency, which allows teams to operate with focus, which itself leads to greater chances for business success.

Sometimes It's OK to Turn the Devices Off

Out on the water, we have a few different ways to communicate. Most recreational sailors generally rely on their cellphones and marine VHF radio, but as they move further away from land, communication with other vessels and with rescue organizations might require satellite radio. There's also an entire language for flags and buoys, and there is also Morse code and semaphore.

These communication methods all require training in their usage—not only in how to use them but also when.

I would never advocate turning off your radio while you're out on the water, but within the more stable scenario of the workplace, turning off your communication technologies temporarily makes good sense and should be encouraged. In fact, one of the greatest misconceptions about using collaboration technology to increase productivity is that they must be on and attended to at all times.

It is a fundamental misconception to believe that collaboration tools must be always on.

It is important to keep pace. When navigating a long journey, maintaining a constant speed is far better than sprinting and resting. When leaders bring their teams close to burnout, those teams, many times, become unrecoverable, and that can cost the business a fortune.

When everything is high priority, that's the same as not having a priority. When team members feel they must be answerable to their communication devices at all times, part of their skill and talent is removed. Those very attributes that you scanned for so carefully during the hiring process and nurtured during their onboarding and development get pushed aside. There are three main ways this can happen:

First, there is the obvious: the fact that people can't focus on their work when they are being interrupted by emails, notifications, phone calls, and chat messages.

Next, there is the distraction factor. The human thinking brain (the logical side, not the emotional side) thrives on focus and does not like to be disturbed. Every time a message comes in, like an email or an instant message, the brain is forced to put all that thinking aside and deal with the urgency of that message.

It's not the content of the message that makes it urgent; it's simply its arrival, disturbing the train of thought—it's a context switch. This is a physiological fact: blood, which is the fuel delivery system for the brain, gets moved quickly away from the "thinking" areas of the brain to the "urgency" centers whenever there is a distraction that is instinctively perceived as an urgency. This blood, and the nutrients and oxygen it carries, does not return to the thinking areas quite as quickly, which means, every time you get interrupted, your brain gets drained of the fuel it needs, and it takes a long time—up to five or maybe ten minutes—for it to come back to full "refueling." This happens every time there's an interruption.

Third, there is the stress of being "on call." People often think of "on call" being only applied to emergency responders, like firefighters, doctors, nurses, or engineers in charge of high-priority IT or machinery. But in actual fact, anyone who is placed in a position of being expected to respond to a message the moment it arrives falls into this same category and suffers the same type of stress-induced fatigue.

When people know that a message can come in at any time, they move to an instinctive level of preparedness, which again prioritizes reaction over proaction. Even if no message actually comes in, the energy of preparedness is spent anyway, and that is energy diverted from other intellectual processes. This in turn leads to a subpar level of ability, through no fault of our own.

One thing at a time. Context switching is expensive.

To develop and encourage high-performance teams, it is better to establish a culture in which people can turn their communication and collaboration devices off once in a while, in order to get some self-directed work done. It's physically easy to do. Every technology has some type of off switch, a mute, or an "out of office" status built into it somewhere. So turning it off is possible physically, but the difficulty is social. People need to feel they have the permission to do this. They need to know that when they turn off their devices temporarily in order to focus, there won't be repercussions.

The answer is simple: if you want people to attain and maintain high levels of performance, you must leave them to focus their talents on their work and prioritize the messaging for later. It's easy to do this: all you—or they—need to learn is how to manage people's expectations. This is done simply by letting other people, team members or even customers, know when they will be responded to, instead of letting these people ride roughshod over the day.

Instruct your people how to manage other people's expectations by giving them a frame of reference. An easy one is "I usually reply to my emails within two hours." This is a message—a streamlining guideline that gives the sender of the original messages relief and comfort, knowing their needs will be met soon.

I use "two hours" as an example. It doesn't have to be two hours in everyone's case. I have known people who state, "I will return your emails by end of day" or "within 24 hours." The time window can be what you want it to be and might even change daily. The point is that you are managing the expectations of the sender by giving them a frame of reference.

That, by the way, is what asynchronous communication is supposed to be about. It's not supposed to be live, like a phone call. It's about keeping a train of communication going, but not *live*. Of course there can be exceptions to this rule, since real emergencies do happen. But in general, this approach to managing people's expectations encourages focus, reduces the negative impact of interruptions, and removes that sense of "on call stress."

Asynchronous communication should be a positive tool of collaboration, not an interruption. Being forced to answer immediately means it's not really asynchronous. Management should always give its blessing to the power of asynchronous communication by actually saying, "It's OK to turn it off and reply later."

Asynchronous communication should be the prevailing medium.

Going back to our time allocation chart in Chapter 8 for a moment, remember that *Collaboration Time* represents the time slots that have been agreed to by the team members as being most convenient for synchronous communication.

Other than that, asynchronous communication should be the prevailing medium, and it should be assigned to the *Catch-up* periods, not responded to immediately.

Thinking in Dotted Lines

Having no process can be just as bad as having too much process, in the same way that with sailing, having no wind can be as bad as having too much wind. Similarly, a good process helps talented people to get more done, while a bad process tries to make up for low accountability.

Having no process is as bad as having too much.

Finding the balance is a challenge. But that's where leaders must direct their talents, and it's what team members should be regularly encouraged to pursue. To build high-performance teams and especially high-performance distributed teams, leaders must establish guidelines that work like dotted lines on a chart, lines that are clear and comprehensible, but not solid and inflexible.

I think of dotted lines as a systematized way to communicate and flag issues in an effective manner. The opposite of a dotted line is either nothing or a strong, bold, and inflexible line. The dotted line is a guide, but it's also a symbol of empowerment. It encourages sufficient flexibility for team members to continually challenge the status quo and to perpetually sharpen people's perspectives on actions.

A dotted line carries with it the message that people should be empowered to identify improvements, come up with their own ideas to make things better, and take actions accordingly. That's fundamental to the continuous improvement mindset, and it is also fundamental to creating an environment where people can innovate. Here's an example:

Your leadership team has given you the *high-level coordinates* to come up with ideas to innovate your product and beat the competition, but with no concrete answers or predefined route. The term high-level coordinates is a dotted line. Acting upon it requires some assessment and decision-making on the part of the individual. It also requires collaboration with other team members without losing sight of the North Star.

A dotted line can be rife with danger. To use it correctly, a team needs help and training to prioritize the risks, categorize and communicate the various levels of severity, and then enact the necessary responses to each. Dotted lines require trust, which is the foundation of the culture of empowerment. *Dotted lines* are as much a team effort as is following them.

Let's revisit my "32 gigs of memory" story from Chapter 8 for a moment. How easy would it have been—in fact, how easy *should it have been*—for us to go ahead and purchase that extra memory, crossing over the dotted line in the interest of demonstrable benefit to the team and the company? Why were we held in place by a procedural anchor?

Remembering That North Star

Remember again what this chapter is about. The North Star is a company's guiding light. It reflects the principles and core values of the organization, and like the actual North Star in the sky, it should be a wholly reliable tool of navigation.

But even out on the water, it is up to the captain and the crew to orient to that star using judgment, experience, and flexibility and also using an uncluttered, non-wasteful process, with flexible dotted lines clearly visible on the map. If the shortest path means you must sail directly over rocks, through a storm, or inside an exclusion zone identified by marker buoys, then it will no longer be the shortest path. If the only person who knows these rules is the captain, who has handed over the helm to another crew member and has gone below decks to rest, then the knowledge is useless.

Too often, organizations veer off course. They lose sight of their North Star largely due to the urgency of the moment. Frankly, it can be difficult to find the time to review these lofty goals when there is day-to-day work to be done. But that's what the essence of great management is: it's about ensuring time is allotted for effective and thorough *planning* and *communication*, those two words that I identified earlier as the core of successful project management.

Case Study: Netflix

Netflix is a great example of how to maximize "North Star success" by using a philosophy of "context rather than control." As a company that pivoted with the changing winds of home entertainment, shifting from sending DVDs in the mail through to taking a dominant position in the *audience-of-one* on-demand streaming model, it not only helped eliminate its early competition such as Blockbuster Video but it has also progressed beyond being just a server of content. Its AI-based algorithms for helping customers find interesting choices have done for home entertainment what Amazon did for shopping. In addition, Netflix has become a creator of its own content, funding and producing groundbreaking series to appeal to the new and fast-growing social trend called binge-watching. In doing this, Netflix essentially elbowed many of the traditional movie production houses out of the way.

To help drive its success, Netflix empowers its employees in ways that are still vastly underused elsewhere. Netflix employees are given the freedom to take risks, and they are not assessed by the number of hours worked but by outcomes.[2]

Another truly awesome resource is available in their Netflix Culture PowerPoint presentation. It's 125 slides long, but every slide is worth reading, and each contains only a sentence or two or a straightforward graph. It is powerful as a 125-slide summary because each slide has something amazing to say.[3]

Earlier in this chapter, I stated that "having no process can be just as bad as having too much process, in the same way that with sailing, having no wind can be as bad as having too much wind." Netflix has a similar approach. They state that "good" process helps talented people to get more done, whereas "bad" process tries to prevent recoverable mistakes. Of particular interest to me is that one of their examples of "bad process" is "getting ten people to interview each candidate," something I touch upon in the next chapter.

There are so many worthwhile quotes in their manifesto and their PowerPoint presentation. Perhaps the one that speaks loudest to me is their vacation policy which is to not have a vacation policy, since "you don't need a policy for everything." How amazing is that? They state "there is also no clothing policy at Netflix, but no one comes to work naked."

This North Star statement is an impressive demonstration of trust and empowerment. I can imagine how many managers would read the Netflix vacation non-policy and immediately think, *What if an employee takes advantage of this and does nothing but claim vacation days?* Such a statement actually proves the power of the Netflix North Star: when you give people the freedom and the respect to leave, when you demonstrate trust in such open amounts, it will actually compel greater loyalty and commitment. And this manifesto is not coming from a brand-new startup filled with ideas but little real-world experience; this comes from Netflix, a company that has changed the world of entertainment delivery, has been around since 1997, and is a regular case study topic for business analysts everywhere.

This trust factor that embodies their vacation non-policy is a vital component that should be factored into any company's own distributed teams manifesto, not for vacations, per se, but as an essential approach to empowerment.

---

[2]Retrieved from Netflix.com. `https://jobs.netflix.com/culture`
[3]All references in this section to the Netflix manifest PowerPoint are from `www.slide-share.net/reed2001/culture-1798664/64-Good_versus_Bad_Process_Good`

The impressive Netflix manifesto is also freely available to read on their website,[4] and given the nautical analogies that I am using, I particularly love quoting this passage:

> If you want to build a ship, don't drum up the people to gather wood, divide the work, and give orders.
>
> Instead, teach them to yearn for the vast and endless sea.

Key Takeaways

- Empowerment gives team members the ability to do their work better and to improve the process at the same time.

- Dotted lines allow for flexibility, which is better routed toward a streamlined process.

- Empowering team members allows them to see and adhere to North Star principles and helps generate a culture of excellence.

---

[4]https://jobs.netflix.com/culture

Opening the Net: Building a Distributed Team

I work in Manhattan, and I live reasonably close by, in the suburbs—Westchester, to be exact. You would think that working in one of the largest and most exciting cities in the world would mean that finding great talent to join a team would be easy. But it's not, and there's more than one reason why.

First, New York City is extremely large, and it sits in the center of a megalopolis that stretches from Boston to Washington D.C., and that means there are a great many companies all looking for talented people. So, with proportionally more employers competing for fewer skilled workers, you get a classic supply and demand challenge. The dominant mindset is still one that says a company must have brick-and-mortar (or steel and glass) buildings in the middle of an economic center to be viable and credible.

The second reason why it's hard to find great people in the New York City area is that not everyone wants to live and work here. Although it's an amazing place to visit, it is also very expensive to live anywhere near it, and it's not everyone's cup of tea.

© Alberto S. Silveira Jr. 2021
A. S. Silveira Jr., *Building and Managing High-Performance Distributed Teams*,
https://doi.org/10.1007/978-1-4842-7055-4_10

But that doesn't matter anymore. This book is about building high-performance distributed teams, and the fact that I can talk about this at all is because people are discovering that working in a distributed team is entirely possible for a variety of jobs. If your work can be done mostly with the assistance of a connected computer, the odds are better than ever that you can do that work from a satellite office (including your own home) as part of a distributed team.

The lockdown of 2020 further demonstrated its viability for knowledge workers, and with virtual reality, augmented reality, and robotics, there is a distinct possibility that "hands-on workers" in a growing range of industries will also be soon able to do some or all of their work in a distributed fashion, from home or from anywhere that provides the appropriate work conditions.

Teachers, too, need to get ready for a continuous shift in teaching methods that includes a greater amount of virtual activity. This latter example was thoroughly field tested during 2020 with mixed results, showing that additional refinements to the process of teaching and learning are needed.

But just because we are not there yet doesn't mean we can't get there. The concept of blended and online education is a North Star in its own right.

Hiring the Best People and Making Efficient Decisions

The people who can best help build your product won't necessarily come from an iconic spot on the map like midtown Manhattan or Silicon Valley. Indeed, the only space you have in common might be online. I have known this instinctively since the earliest days of my career and even before that, when I was organizing my local soccer teams, but it is being proven more correct with each passing day.

If I want to hire the best talent, I will hire them regardless of where they are physically and also without regard for their ability to fit into the standard nine-to-five convention that defined and dictated work habits in earlier decades. I strongly believe that leaders should "open the net" and adapt to a new normal in which the best talent might live somewhere beyond the traditional one-to-two-hour commuting radius of the central office.

This means I need a streamlined hiring process that is efficient and engaging for the candidate, not just for me. Great talents often have multiple job offers in front of them, so agility is key to the process. Even those who do not have additional job offers know that communication and collaboration technologies have vastly opened up the concept of career mobility.

I believe it is part of my responsibility as a leader in attracting the right people and in building high-performance distributed teams to know that these people are free to find something more appealing at any time. It makes me want to work harder to ensure the culture and the work are a right fit for each individual.

Hiring the best talent from wherever they are requires a new way of thinking. Many leaders often overthink, and they struggle to make decisions within the traditional model. It's a type of thinking that gets absorbed into a person's professional soul as time goes by, one that gets dominated by process rather than substance. This type of thinking tends to overinflate everything: project plans, planning of the plans, holding synchronous meetings, and producing copious amounts of all types of back-and-forth messages.

Hiring the best talent from wherever they are requires a new way of thinking.

Compare this to the bowtie model of Iron Triangle process management described in Chapter 5. Part of this was to identify the ideal size for smart and efficient decision-making, which comes down to empowering three people (inbound or outbound) with different perspectives to collaborate and collectively make more educated decisions.

Traditional leaders and managers come from a legacy process that involves thinking too much about the wrong things and sticking to protracted interview processes and inefficient decision-making approaches, including making decisions by committee. There is an old expression that says, "A camel is a horse designed by a committee," and it's true to this day. When every single person around the table has to say "yes" in order to bring a new person on board, that's a challenge. It's always difficult to get everyone to agree, and the more people involved, the more problematic and time-consuming that process becomes.

Large blue chip companies might interview a hundred people and still struggle with the decision to hire a great talent simply because they failed to get unanimity. In other words, "not every interviewer said 'yes,' so we went with 'no.'" To be fair, when many of these companies developed their interview process, the world was a different place. Even ten years ago it was a different place.

Naturally, the hiring manager should collect the data from the other interviewers, collect references, and use those data points to make a more educated decision. However, that shouldn't require long meetings with every interviewer in order to reach a unanimous agreement. At the end of the day, the hiring manager should be the decision-maker, accountable for individual performance as well as team performance. Empowerment, accountability, and failure are all necessary ingredients to build a strong team.

Not being able to hire the best talent quickly is what I identify as an *opportunity cost* to the business. As I like to say to my hiring managers, making no decision is often worse than making the wrong decision. Make a decision, evaluate quickly, and fail fast. Failure is part of the process to achieve success. Learn from it and keep moving forward.

Failure is part of the process to achieve success.

One of My Own Fail Fast Examples

In my early days at a previous company, I made a referral for a person with whom I had worked a decade earlier. I was excited to be able to refer to this individual. I felt that this person was eminently qualified—both in terms of skills and trustworthiness, but also for what I knew about this person. The referral was for a position that reported directly to me, but I made sure that the person went through the full interview process with the team regardless. Long story short, the whole team gave their thumbs-up for the candidate. We all thought the person would be a great fit.

Approximately ten weeks later, I made the decision to fire this person. I realized I had made a mistake in understanding this individual's ability to gel with the team and the work, and I also observed a significant inability or reluctance on the part of this person to respond to constructive feedback. The team was shocked at how quickly this happened, but was not entirely surprised that it did. It was a difficult decision for me, especially because I had known this person for over ten years.

In this particular hiring exercise, I failed. But I made sure to fail fast and learn from it. What I learned was that just because I had known this person for such a long time, this should not have influenced my judgment as to the person being a good fit for the role. My team also learned that expectations for each role apply to everyone, regardless of where they come from.

As difficult as this was, I also learned that it gained me even more respect from the team members who saw my dedication to keeping the bar of quality high, allowing the team to continue to push it higher. My devotion to the team's overall success, even at the cost of a long friendship, resonated with the team members.

The Right People Aboard

I prefer to work with, or for, a mission-driven organization, one that knows it will have meaning and a positive impact on people's lives, and I feel that people who have chosen to work in a distributed teams setup usually have that freedom of spirit. They embody my *One Team, One Heart* way of leading, following, and innovating. The best talent likes to work for a purpose. They like to know they are connecting with something worthwhile, and yes, they like to be acknowledged for their efforts.

Healthy teams aren't built in a day. But they are built each day.

Acknowledgement for one's efforts does not always mean money. Although most people must work to pay their bills, most of the time money is not the primary motivating factor that attracts or retains great people to great teams. Things like quality of culture, work-life balance and flexibility, supportive leadership, creative and engaging environments, the appreciation of the people they have around them, and overall respect are on the top of the list in many *best places to work* survey results. None of these things are about money. But they underscore the importance of working with the passions of your team members and giving them the chance to grow and be aligned to the North Star.

In my sailing life, I never thought I would end up crewing on a racing sailboat full of Hungarians off the coast of Croatia. And they certainly did not hire me because I just happened to be sitting there on the dock, next to the boat. The circumstances that pulled me to that team came from a combination of other factors. I had to have the skills, energy, and the passion for the position in the crew that they were looking to fill, but I also had to have the attitude and the desire to win. My inability to speak Hungarian—in other words, being a precise fit for the position as described—was not a deal-breaker. My willingness to embrace the culture and the vision of the team made me a viable candidate. The desire to win is what makes the difference between average teams and high-performance teams.

So it goes with every effort that focuses on bringing the right people aboard. There are many elements that go into the decision, but few of them will demand exact conformity to a predefined shape. Instead decision-making should be about thinking creatively and seeking widely; empowering hiring managers to make decisions and be accountable for them; finding people aligned with your culture and mission; finding people with the requisite skills, certainly, but, more importantly, people who are open-minded and willing to learn; and finding people with the attitude to make things happen and who have passion and who can align to the mission.

We Don't Need to Scale Up to the Enterprise Mindset

There are companies out there that have grown so large and so globally widespread that their team-building, interviewing, and onboarding processes have become mechanized and impersonal. I know this from first-hand experience. I interviewed at three of the largest and best-known high-tech companies on the planet, each time for senior-level positions. What I found was, as sophisticated and well-engineered as their recruiting, interviewing, hiring, and onboarding processes were, they seemed, to me at least, to substantially lack the trust and the human aspect I was looking for. There's a difference between joining a company and getting excited to be part of one. If you have to read one or multiple books to be prepared to pass an interview, we are all missing something.

Hire people based on who they are rather than just what they can do.

As I have already mentioned, I look for people who are mission-driven and who have the ability to weave our company's North Star values into their ideas and actions. They show me daily that they are not just working for a paycheck. I regularly refer back to a book I have read a couple of times now, called *Who: The A Method for Hiring*, by Geoff Smart and Randy Street. Their process aligns with mine in terms of observing potential team members for who they are, instead of just "what they can do."

Smart and Street explain that once you understand who a person is, you can start to get a sense of their problem solving skills and their overall passion for the line of business you are trying to build. Yes, there will still be conversations during the interview and hiring process, but as much as possible, the interview should focus on the human aspect.

As a result of my own experiences, supported by the expertise of people like Smart and Street, I know I typically don't need to interview 20 or 30 people to find the right candidate for a job. That's a good thing because interviewing is expensive and time-consuming. You could argue that the cost of interviewing, both in terms of money and time, is merely the cost of doing business, or the cost of due diligence. I would agree with that, but only if the activity of interviewing 20 or 30 people is demonstrably necessary. If it is not, but instead, it has simply become part of a static process, then it has little value.

And really, when would this be necessary? If I had to interview more than five to ten people for a given position, I think I would need to revisit my interview process. Is my job description even aligned with the expectations for the job? Do I even know what I'm looking for? One key aspect while interviewing is to have a process in place that allows a consistent approach to analyzing candidates. Another key aspect is to learn after each interview cycle and identify opportunities to make the process more efficient. This will result in a better experience not only for the candidates but also for the team members who are investing their time interviewing people.

When companies reach a certain size, they—ironically—run out of internal resources to make things happen in an agile way. It becomes more natural for these companies to drift back into a command-and-control mode where "just do it" becomes the natural call to make. The culture of "just do it" then cascades down through the hierarchy and through the chain of command, completely bypassing, for instance, the empowerment that Iron Triangle leadership brings to the table and instead limiting people and teams to innovate and do their best resulting in frustration.

In today's economy, there isn't the time or tolerance for this type of management. There's no question that building great teams is vital to an organization, but leaders of small organizations should do themselves a favor and stop mimicking traditional big enterprise practices—not only now, when they are small, but later too, when they grow.

This is why I like the fail fast idea. When describing SpaceX in Chapter 4, I made mention of their fail-forward approach. I always found that to be an interesting concept. When interviewing candidates, I have always liked its variation, the "fail-fast" approach, meaning "learn, improve, repeat." This is also the basis of the Deming Cycle that I mention in more detail in Chapter 12. Quite simply, from a hiring perspective, "fail-forward" eliminates the need and the pressure to find the exact match from a field of candidates through traditional, extensive, long interview processes, and instead to find someone who appears to fit the culture and then work on developing that person, in line with their personal passions and the North Star, as a process of continuous improvement going forward.

Freelancers and the Gig Economy

It has been suggested by high-ranking consulting firms, industry experts, and even the World Economic Forum that the future of work will rely a great deal on freelancers working the "gig economy" with estimates going as far as to suggest that up to 50 percent of the US workforce will be freelance by 2027.[1]

---

[1] World Economic Forum: www.weforum.org/agenda/2017/12/predictions-for-freelance-work-education/

For many decades, the concept of the *freelancer* conjured up one of two types of people: either the self-sufficient "gun for hire" like a professional photographer who will shoot the company catalog, get paid, and disappear again or the scornful stereotype of the ne'er-do-well who just doesn't seem able to hold down a real job.

It's a shame that most people who freelance are lumped into this second category. I also take issue with this concept of a *real job*. This is an outdated notion, and as we have seen through many economic boom and bust cycles, having a nine-to-five job at an established company is no guarantee of permanent prosperity. A *real job* is what you do to pay the bills, create some degree of security, and find opportunities for satisfaction and, if desired, advancement. This should differ for every individual and should be defined solely by them. It might even require wearing many hats.

Freelancers really deserve more respect, especially in this era and especially when it comes to high-performance distributed teams. They are trained to adapt and are comfortable with constant change. They are also great at making sure their skills remain up-to-date and forming or joining temporary teams. They are to the skilled workforce economy what SaaS (software as a service) companies are to technology. They are part of the new as-a-service mindset, in which the responsibility for self-maintenance and self-improvement is taken on by the as-a-service companies and individuals themselves, and the delivery of their services is based on a proactive, modular, as-needed basis.

The term *freelance* is another one of those words that have a delightful historical pedigree. It was originally a medieval term for a mercenary soldier, whose chief weapon (their lance) was not affiliated with any army and was free to be hired by whichever lord or monarch needed it. In the meantime, it was up to each individual mercenary to keep their skills and tools up-to-date and ready.

The future belongs to those who know how to find customers and deliver great work on an as-a-service basis.

This gives you two nonexclusive choices for building your distributed team. One is to get in with great freelancers, pulling them into your teams as needed. They are already adept at delivering quality from wherever they might be, geographically, on the planet. It helps when freelancers, like any other type of distributed team members, share some things in common, including time zones and a strong amount of cultural and industry awareness, but their agility, accessibility, reliability, and focus on quality are their stock-in-trade.

Even if your preference is to build your distributed teams out of the people who are already employees of the company, but who are becoming part of the ever-growing "work from wherever" culture, it is a good idea to bring freelancers into the fold, to observe how they do what they do, and to integrate some of their talent and versatility into the company's own culture.

One Team

When I have encountered freelancers and contractors in some of the organizations I have worked with, I have seen a mostly wasted resource. Despite all the positive, proactive attributes about freelancers that I just described, they are often treated as external elements. They are not allowed to connect with the corporate community or its North Star. They are, in fact, treated much like the offshore workers I described in Chapter 3, even if they are physically sitting in your building.

I prefer to call freelancers and contractors *third-party partners*, and this isn't simple window dressing. I walk this walk and talk this talk. I want these people, whose own mission is to hone their skills and be as professionally excellent as possible, to align with the company's mission. I want to bring them to company meetings. I want them to attend departmental social events. I want them to be no different than any other full-time team member. I want them to live the spirit of inclusion. I want every team member to feel as *One Team, One Heart*.

I want every team member to feel as One Team, One Heart.

In Chapter 8, I mentioned the practicality of using prefixes and suffixes in chat apps and emails as a method of streamlining communication just like Seaspeak. So it surprises me when I see large companies whose own Seaspeak includes adding the letter X to every freelancer/contractor's email address and online identification for labor law purposes. Why an X? Why not a plus sign +? That might seem like a small pedantic observation, but is it really? To me an X stands for "wrong" or "ex-something." Its connotations are largely negative or subtractive, whereas a + is largely positive or additive. As a component of business language, such a simple change can have a huge impact on seeing freelancers as extraneous or included. This in turn will affect the performance of the individuals as well as those on the team who work with them.

This concept expands to the larger difference between building a product and doing projects. The product is an inclusive concept consisting of many people and activities, focused on the North Star. Projects are individualized activities that are more easily segmented yet which still have an alignment to the North Star. The individual projects have a symbolic connection to the individual members of the team, whether these are employees or freelancers. That is the goal, of course, but I have seen so many projects lose their connection with the North Star because people see the project as simply a "point in time."

Leaders will often decide to hire freelancers or contractors exclusively for specific projects that somehow couldn't get prioritized along with the others. When such projects, along with the people who work on them, are viewed in isolation, this might indeed result in talent, resources, and money being applied to genuinely less important things at the expense of a broader-scale pursuit of the North Star.

Freelancers and contractors have a great deal to contribute to traditional office-centric or distributed teams. As a leader you must be able and willing to rely on them, which means trusting them. You must be willing to include them as part of the team completely. This includes making them part of all of the meetings and decision-making discussions that any other full-time employee would join and participate in and giving them access to what they need to perform their jobs well. The point is to create an environment where there are no differences and where everyone in the team operates and lives united. That is the *One Team, One Heart* spirit.

Distributed Teams Operate on Trust and Outcomes

If you are considering hiring or building a distributed team, the next question should be, "How do you know that people within the distributed team are operating at their best capacity and at the right pace?"

Often, managers who dislike the concept of distributed teams are mistrustful of the employees, imagining that they will spend their days slacking off, surfing on the Internet, or doing chores around the house. I dislike that attitude because mistrust adds poison to the atmosphere, which makes the formation of a high-performance team next to impossible. It's a self-fulfilling prophecy. Managers who show distrust to their employees set the stage for a relationship of further mutual distrust, which leads to subpar performance and high turnover.

By contrast, when you seek out people who love the work they do, who have been selected to join the team based on *who* they are, and who experience an atmosphere of trust, respect, and positivity, it's often difficult to get them to actually stop working. People are great that way. They take pride in doing great work and are energized by being given the chance to show what they can do. I would venture to say that in most of the cases where a manager has a "bad apple," that unmotivated employee who confirms a manager's worst fears about trust and delegation, it's not that person who is the problem, but that the job they are in is not a match to who they are.

To me the best way to determine if distributed teams are working is to focus on outcomes, rather than watching every move a person makes. This is described in more detail in Chapter 7.

Determining Results in a Distributed Team

How do you define and obtain results in the workplace? In Chapter 2, I mentioned how face time is still considered by many managers as a key indicator of performance, although I fail to see how. Just because a person is present at work in the office and looks like they are working doesn't mean that work is getting done in the right way or in the right amounts.

This is not always the team member's fault, by the way. Again, very few people seriously want to coast through their jobs. But the at-work workplace can become an obstacle to productivity, due to its many distractions. This is, again, why time management education is in such high demand and equally why Lean management principles, including concepts such as *Muda, Mura, and Muri*, are necessary in a production environment.

What most managers seem to value most about face time and keeping work on the premises is that they can hold meetings, check that the team members are working, and drop in to chat with them whenever they want. But none of these things guarantee optimum productivity.

The distributed teams model offers the best of both worlds, in terms of giving people the flexibility to work in isolation when needed, but also to have direct connection through synchronous communication as well.

Deliverables—the actual work produced by team members—need to be defined and quantified, usually around an axis of customer value, not by hours clocked in. But they can and should remain flexible enough to fit into each employee's specific set of work requirements and be aligned more closely to their own circadian rhythms. For example, when a product manager wants to add a new feature to the product, they would write down the expected outcomes as the requirements instead of prescribing the solution. How this work is done should be up to the individuals that will implement the solution itself. This is trust and empowerment combined. If someone wishes to do this self-directed work between 1:00 a.m. and 4:00 a.m., who is anyone to say "no" so long as the quality and the end product meet the desired outcomes?

I believe much more in people's individual passion and energy as a reliable high-performance fuel. Much greater synergy can be generated among people who know they are respected and supported and who work in an environment that readily conforms to their personal selves, both physically, through technology, and also culturally through proactive, high-touch management. I want to give people the motivation to make the work happen, because then I can be sure they have put their heart and soul into it. This is not a theoretical exercise. It is not just a matter of believing in this—it has been proven many times: empowered people reliably deliver better results.

Empowered people reliably deliver better results.

And once again, repetition is key. At the start of Chapter 9, I described the New York City Subway system's mantra of "if you see something, say something." So now is a good time to expand upon this statement and place it in the workplace.

The "say something" concept is not a command. It's permission. It's encouragement. It's empowerment. It's not just about what might be said; it's about a shared ownership of a process and solution. If there is a better way to do something, employees should be encouraged to do it that way. Try it out. If there is an opportunity for innovation, that should be shared with the team. When people share such items, they also share the culture.

Turning the Career Ladder into the Career Vine

Let's imagine you are looking to hire someone for your team. If you're in IT, maybe you are thinking you need to hire someone who knows the Java programming language. If you're opening a company that supplies quality foods to restaurants, maybe you think you need to hire a chef or a cook who has worked in a restaurant or two.

Maybe. But I prefer to not hire people based on that type of reasoning. Instead, I prefer to hire people based on how much they can learn, what they have done in their past experiences, and what they say they can contribute the most to the business. I place less focus on the tools or technology they used. In my field of software products, for example, what's the point of looking for a PHP or Java specialist? What I need is to be able to offer a learning-enabled environment in which continuous improvement and continuous learning are constantly promoted. I want someone who is technology agnostic and who is interested in the business and is willing and able to learn and adapt as needed.

Earlier I talked about the super-complex interview process that some organizations employ, sometimes sifting through hundreds of résumés to find that one person who matches the job as described. But what if the job does not turn out to be what was described?

This to me epitomizes the difference between hiring someone for an existing job and hiring someone to join a company on a quest, in which learning, communication, and passion—belief in the North Star and in cultural alignment—are vital for every person in every position. This is about hiring to match a culture of change and innovation rather than exclusively to match for an existing job posting.

I am not alone in this. The *Cybersecurity Workforce Study*, published in December 2020 by the International Information System Security Certification Consortium, also known as (ISC)2, highlighted a significant deficit in cybersecurity. It stated that around 3.1 million professionals are needed to bridge the cybersecurity talent gap—a growth factor of 89 percent. That's just one industry—cybersecurity. What is key, though, is that the report shows how excessive requirements for hiring, including years of experience, professional certifications, plus inflated expectations for junior roles, are the problem, rather than an actual lack of workers.

(ISC)2 as well as other cybersecurity organizations suggest that greater focus should be placed on hiring people from diverse, nontraditional backgrounds, with ongoing training replacing high barriers to entry. This is what I have always stood for, and I am glad to see it being recognized by associations like (ISC)2 that oversee professional education and certification in this industry.[2]

I like to hire people who are smarter than me, people who have better or different approaches. And I am not the first person to have said this. One visionary who said it best put it like this: "It doesn't make sense to hire smart people and tell them what to do; we hire smart people so they can tell us what to do." The visionary was Steve Jobs, and his legacy speaks for itself. But he, too, was not the only person to voice this sentiment. Another of my favorite sayings, which has been attributed to people across history from Confucius to Elon Musk, is, "If you are the smartest person in the room, then you're in the wrong room." It just makes sense. Give people the space to excel and they will, often in ways you never expected.

What you'll find is that the career trajectory that individual team members take is seldom connected to the interview process or to the rules and expectations set during onboarding. It's much more of an organic thing, a vine rather than a ladder. This might be new to many people who have been in the workplace for more than two decades. The degree of flexibility and career mobility that people can enjoy today should be seen as an asset, not a threat.

Frankly, I want to attract people who know they are good enough to work in a range of companies and industries. I consider it my obligation and challenge to make a workplace culture that is sufficiently attractive for that kind of person. As an addition to the Netflix examples I shared in the previous chapter, I think also of the words of Richard Branson, a visionary who has been bucking the corporate mindset trend for decades, who said it best:

Train people well enough so they can leave. Treat them well enough so they don't want to.

---

[2]Retrieved from (ISC)2. www.isc2.org/Research/-/media/0AAF29023217474EB5D0D7 6170A75ABB.ashx

Key Takeaways

- The best people might no longer exist within traditional commuting belts. They will be available within the distributed teams structure.

- All people should feel part of the team and aligned to the North Star. This includes freelancers and contractors as much as employees.

- The best people know they can work elsewhere. This should be considered an opportunity, not a threat. It's a leader's job to make them want to stay.

Staying Shipshape

The Importance of Tracking Mood

Some will say it's not possible for a body of water to display human attributes like anger or joy, but anyone who has spent any time on the water knows it is indeed capricious and full of personality and spirit. How could it not be? It is also full of life, and we humans are 70 percent water. We share an ancient connection that goes far beyond mere sight and touch.

Similarly, I love to observe and also measure the mood of people. Becoming aware of mood and learning to understand it is one of those soft skills that the future-of-work experts highlight as essential. Some people factor this into the school of thought called emotional intelligence or organizational awareness. Understanding the mood of a team and of its individual members is vital.

Moods have enormous influence on productivity and relationships, and they are also contagious. Human beings spend a lot of their time subconsciously reading the moods of others by observing body language, subtle gestures,

© Alberto S. Silveira Jr. 2021
A. S. Silveira Jr., *Building and Managing High-Performance Distributed Teams*,
https://doi.org/10.1007/978-1-4842-7055-4_11

eye contact, tone of voice, timing of reactions, and verbal mannerisms, which all have enormous power in what they convey.

We have all been tripped up on occasion by a poorly worded email or text message whose meaning might be colored not by the writer's intent but by the recipient's mood. Think about a one-word reply from your boss, colleague, or significant other. What if this one-word message said "Fine" or, worse, "Whatever." With a message that short, you have little to go on in terms of interpreting its true meaning. You will turn to your own mood along with any level of worry, guilt, or anger that you carry in your relationship with the sender. This is an inadvertent prejudice that cannot fail to further inflame these words into negative connotations even when none was intended. That's the problem with a sterile medium like text messaging. It can fall prey so easily to misunderstanding.

Within any group of people, mood can be extremely contagious, and this runs across the entire spectrum, from fear and panic on one side to calm, optimism, and happiness on the other. Mood is an energy that over time, and in the larger context of a team, we often define as *morale*. It becomes the fuel for a team, influencing every action and interaction.

Why Mood Is More Powerful Than Intellect

As human beings, we might pride ourselves on our intellect—we belong to the species *Homo sapiens*, which is Latin for "wise person." But we are not that wise. We may have learned a lot, and we may know a lot, but we are still more heavily influenced by emotion than logic.

We are more influenced by emotion than by logic.

The most powerful emotion of all is fear, and that's a good thing, generally, since fear is primarily responsible for keeping us alive, by seeking to avoid dangerous situations. But that fear also tends to smother our intellectual side and has been—and continues to be—the cause of a great many of our problems.

The debate over the use of masks and social distancing during the pandemic is a classic case of how these emotions can completely mess us up. The virus was an invisible threat, as compared to, say, a person holding a gun. As such it required intellect to understand the nature of its threat and especially the nature of its contagion potential, which epidemiologists call its r factor. Although scientists might have hoped that the instinctive fear of death would prevail, it was instead the fear of change, which led to acts of outright resistance and denial in many countries, furthering the spread of infection and death into the millions.

Since emotion is so powerful and has such a direct impact on the mood of a team, it must be tracked, using metrics in league with observation, insight, and intuition.

Some managers like to observe the mood in their teams by polling them: offering surveys, asking for continuous feedback, holding internal focus groups, town halls, and one-on-one discussions. These are all especially useful and are never a complete waste of time, but I will always lean toward interaction and the collection of unstructured information as better indicators of individual moods and group moods. To me, context is vital.

Reading the Mood

The most direct and seemingly obvious way to read someone's mood, for example, as a company might do to determine customer satisfaction, is to send out a survey. But there are significant limitations to this approach. Firstly, if a survey is not mandatory, then you will only receive feedback from people whose personality is open to, or feels guilted into, responding to it. Whether you are polling users or a customer base, the data collected will be skewed to reflect the opinions of people who can be influenced to answer polls and will leave out a significantly sized group populated by those whose personality types will not answer a questionnaire request.

Secondly, every question in a questionnaire includes the writer's own bias in the way it is framed and by the answer choices offered. Words like *somewhat* and *strongly* or *almost never* are way too subjective. Some respondents, looking at a scale of 1–10, with 1 being *least satisfied* and 10 being *most satisfied*, will automatically avoid the extremes of 1 and 10 out of a desire to not be considered an extreme person. They might get frustrated by the narrow scope of the questions or even the length of the questionnaire, meaning that anger or impatience might also skew the data.

The best way, in my opinion, to read the mood of a group is to interpret unstructured data. Unstructured data largely appears as paragraphs of words, either spoken or written. For example, if I absolutely had to use a questionnaire to get people's opinions, rather than offer a scale of 1–10 or a yes-or-no answer, I would offer a space for the respondents to write out their thoughts. In a group setting, I would give people a chance to speak uninterrupted. This allows them to verbalize their thoughts in a way that best aligns with their thought processes and their emotions. Also, when someone talks, the act of "letting go" of one thought by sharing it with the interviewer often spurs additional thoughts that would never have come to the surface in a more restrictive, closed-ended questioning scenario.

Another unstructured way to read the mood of a team is through data delivered in the form of notes, essays, emails, or conversations and posts on social media. This is not about snooping; it's about turning to places where people let their thoughts run free in a conversational style. When it comes to external customers, for example, you can learn much more from comments about you or your competitors on a social media platform than you can from a survey.

But the best feedback comes from conversation, and this is something that can be done just as easily through one-on-one video chat as it can in person. Again, this technique is not new. As I mentioned earlier, within the *kaizen* concept of continuous improvement, managers of Japanese factories were encouraged to perform *gemba* walks, which required them to leave their desks and walk around, visiting assembly line workers, talking to them, and even thanking them publicly for doing things that supported continuous improvement, like calling attention to a defect that would require a temporary stoppage of the manufacturing process.

Gemba is not just a demonstration of public respect, even though that would be a sufficient morale booster in itself, it's also an opportunity for managers to hear directly from their frontline employees in their own words. In North America, the equivalent of the *gemba* walk is called MBWA—*management by walking around*. Perhaps it's time for a new term to add to this collection: MBZA—*management by zooming around*.

The secret to *gemba* and MBWA is quite simply to listen more than you speak. When someone is allowed to speak, they will reveal far more than when they are simply allowed to answer a question.

Leaders should create a "psychologically safe" environment where people feel encouraged to share their mood. There is an expectation for things to get better or something new to happen when people share their thoughts. When no action is taken, that often causes frustration. The most important piece of the puzzle in terms of collecting data around people's mood is to understand what has been collected and then take positive and noticeable action.

Reading Flags at Sea

Flags are vital in boating and shipping. They serve as visual, unambiguous messengers that do not rely on languages or radio communication. A red flag with a white diagonal stripe tells boaters that divers are working nearby. An orange flag with a black circle and a black square side by side is the international signal of distress. A flag with red and yellow diagonal triangles means person overboard. These are excellent examples of streamlined communication since every captain and crew member is required to know what to do when they see these flags.

Probably the most famous maritime flag of all is the Jolly Roger, the skull and crossbones on a black background. Well known for being flown by pirates, the legend says that the black background meant a ship would be given "quarter." This told the crews of the ships being approached by the pirates that they would be spared if they let the pirates board and steal what they wanted. This bleak message was enough to elicit compliance even in situations where the pirates themselves would have been hopelessly outnumbered. Once again, fear led the way. The worse news for a crew would be a red pirate flag, which meant no quarter would be given regardless.

Pirates from the seventeenth and eighteenth century are interesting from a team management perspective. Yes, they can be accurately described as opportunistic thieves, but they were not the only ones. There were also privateers—private merchant ships that had a license to engage in plunder and war in support of commerce in the name of their king, queen, or president.

Many pirate ships ran democratically, with each crew member having a vote on the ship's issues, fair distribution of the plunder, and a strong and respectful social culture, which made being part of a pirate crew one of the more attractive places to work at sea. As a consequence, it was common during a pirate raid for the crew members of victim ships to not only step aside but to also ask for a job on the pirate ship itself.

But what was clear was that the flag was an unambiguous and streamlined communication device for the maritime community of that era.

Reading Silence in the Workplace

In terms of team dynamics in the workplace, silence can be dangerous, and that is a warning flag in itself. Many people keep negative emotions including worries or animosity toward others bottled up inside where they fester and grow. But what must be remembered by team leaders is that bad feelings and grudges never go away.

The reason these negative sentiments never disappear is due to the same fear response I described earlier. Bad feeling or disappointment happens when something goes contrary to the way you would like it to go. Your instincts automatically equate that to something that might in itself represent danger. That's one reason why disappointments always last longer and are stronger in memory than good events.

In the workplace, bad feelings and grudges live forever, and they tend to grow with every successive interaction with the person who caused them. This is where interpersonal conflicts arise, usually from long-standing, unrecognized slights. These can happen just as easily in distributed teams as with onsite groups. In both situations, the bad feelings might go undetected for months or years, especially if all communication is cursory and superficial.

As a manager, it is vital to get team members to talk, using the techniques I have already described: one-on-one meetings, *gemba* or MBWA walks, and MBZA. In the previous chapter, I mentioned how the commentaries that people used to describe their "best places to work" revealed how important it is to provide a supportive communication environment that involves unstructured conversation, active listening, and emotional intelligence and how this has such an enormous positive impact on collective mood. Such connection points are vital to the building and nurturing of a successful distributed team, and thankfully the technology exists to make this happen.

Balloons and Gravity

Hot air balloons are impressive devices, but there is one thing about them that must never be forgotten: in the contest between the hot air balloon and gravity, gravity always wins—eventually.

This is important when it comes to understanding mood, because the same applies here too. Collective moods can fall just as easily as they can rise, and the fall is much faster, and its effects are longer-lasting. Some individuals are upbeat and optimistic by nature, others less so, and still others struggle with depression and anxiety. Collectively a team or a crew is going to start out being a mosaic of these personality types, meaning each person in the group remains their own true self, separate and distinct, but over time and with great, proactive management, you can transform the mosaic into something of a *gestalt*, a melting and blending of individuals into a community with a shared mood and clear channels of communication and support. It's genuinely great when this happens. It's a particular synergy that creates an enviable, productive team—almost a family.

Gestalt: The whole is greater than the sum of its parts.

But collective moods, like hot air balloons, need additional energy and maintenance to stay up and to skirt turbulence.

I have seen some companies, who, sensing a dip in morale, send their teams out on one-day team-building exercises, like navigating rope bridges, engaging in trust activities, or spending the afternoon at a ball game. These can be nice, but if the return to work brings with it a corresponding drop in mood, then the "day out" provided nothing to keep the mood afloat for more than a few hours, and the corresponding return to Earth will feel even more profound and heavy. The same would apply to the crew of a ship: a day of shore leave is nice, but if the source of low morale is not addressed, the crew will simply descend back into it as soon as they step back on board.

It remains the duty of the manager or captain to stay aware of the mood of the team, to spot potential emotional storms on the horizon, and to remain aware also of the importance this all has to the mission. It's an act of constant watching and measurement—part of Deming's concept, "you can't manage what you can't measure."

How to Read and Balance Moods in a Distributed Teams Scenario

Understanding how to manage mood is on par with understanding the value of sleep in our lives. Can you imagine living without sleep? It's impossible, and it can actually be fatal. Human beings basically spend one-third of their lives asleep. It would be nice, perhaps, to contemplate a life where it was not needed. Think how much more you would be able to do with all those extra hours and years of wakefulness! But it's foolish to think that way. Healthy sleep is absolutely vital. Without it, you would not be able to function properly during your waking hours. So it's a done deal: one-third of the project that you call your life must be given over to sleep.

At first glance sleep does not seem to achieve anything, but when you look at what it actually entails in terms of dreaming, physical and emotional repair, and rest, it contributes enormously. It's actually quite fascinating.

Managing the morale of your teams has a parallel prerogative. Some managers might not see the value of emotional intelligence and morale management, but these actions deliver the same restorative health-giving benefits to teams as sleep does for the individual human. If proactive team management— including morale management and online *gemba* walks—takes up one-third of your management time, so be it. That's the cost of developing high-performance distributed teams. The other two-thirds of your time will achieve far less without this.

The goal is to understand people's thoughts, concerns, and ideas. Leaders have to be available to their people, and they have to make sure that each person in the team is connected to everything they need to give their best in their area of expertise. Never underestimate what a person with a purpose can achieve.

Never underestimate what a person with a purpose can achieve.

Remove the Formality

One of the best ways to manage mood and morale in a distributed teams scenario is to deformalize the communication technology. Many people turn to video chat apps just when there is a meeting to attend, which is basically a formalized activity. But these communication tools can do so much more. You can establish a dedicated chat channel, like in Slack or Microsoft Teams, to be used for spontaneous hallway chats, quick talks about the weekend, and anything else that you and your team members feel would contribute to a sense of togetherness and casual team building.

The nonformality component of work is vital. One of the key elements of traditional on-premises work is the use of casual space. This includes the cafeteria, lunchroom or food court, hallways, elevators, lobbies, basically anywhere that is related to the company but is not specific to a task or project. This is where people talk and socialize, but more importantly, it is where they reinforce their sense of community and social awareness.

The absence of this drop-in casual space is something that first-time work from home employees observed during the pandemic lockdown. Video chats were used for meetings, and self-directed work was done at home, but little attention was given to the midpoint—that awareness that you are with other people, that they are nearby. This absence is palpable and points to a significant must-have among distributed teams—the social aspect.

It also sets up a perfect triangle of its own that I feel is wholly supportive of any team scenario, whether traditional or distributed: formal work (team meetings and similar scheduled events), self-directed work (research, writing, coding, analysis—basically the tasks that reflect a person's job title), and socialization.

Some might ask why email is not added to this triangle, which is a good question, given how much time email and other messaging techniques take up. But I consider these to be "support activities," necessary, but not primary. It's a sad reality that most people at work have lost control of their emails and are not truly aware of just how much time they must spend each day in managing them. But, as I mention in Chapter 8, this is what Catch-up Time is for. The hallmark of a truly successful team is one where the amount of Catch-up Time required is brought down to a minimum.

It is easy to set up social drop-in spaces using online breakout rooms in video chat apps or even using specialized apps dedicated to this type of casual, spontaneous interaction. The reason these software solutions have not been introduced to the workplace culture is, I believe, because more attention has been given over to the formalized, team-focused side of the triangle (e.g., online synchronous meetings) and because informal socialization in a team environment is much like air—people don't notice it when they are surrounded by it, but they do once it starts to disappear. Socialization is a vital and highly constructive component of any distributed team architecture, and I think we will see a lot more development in this space in the immediate future.

Observing Observability

Take the concept of observability, for example, that I touched upon earlier. In the old, brick-and-mortar postindustrial mindset, the accountability for ensuring that a process ran smoothly and in the right direction would sit squarely on the shoulders of the CEO and a small team of senior managers. Although this seems to be the correct level of authority for oversight, it has the potential to become a classic command-and-control scenario. What is more, executive oversight does not always incorporate real observation. It's more like monitoring—looking only at certain metrics.

These days it is becoming obvious that a better way to make sure the organization is not going on an emotional detour is to make it everyone's responsibility to observe. Observing is a 360-degree activity and is also a team concept and should not belong only to the captain or CEO, and it is definitely not just about watching the numbers or metrics. Observing includes metrics, certainly, but it encompasses a great deal more peripheral vision, instinct, and insight.

It is everyone's responsibility to observe.

Only with a much wider and more comprehensive perspective can things be corrected and improved both when things are going well and when they are not. It is about being able to take decisive actions to implement improvements, even when everything has seemingly reached a state of optimum efficiency.

The Company That Helps People Quit

If you read a headline like this, "the company that helps people quit," the chances are that you will interpret that to mean it's about severance pay, or for setting up *golden parachutes* for executives. But, no, that's not what this is about. I want to tell you a story about a company that knows a thing or two about morale.

The company in question is called Jellyvision, a Chicago-based employee communication software company with about 400 employees. Although it works hard to create a positive community and a legitimately upbeat mood, on occasion, a person decides they no longer want to work there. Perhaps it's a career trajectory thing or a lifestyle change or simply that the company and the industry just isn't a fit for them. That happens sometimes. For whatever reason, they just want to get off this boat.

For most people in this situation, life now becomes a careful tightrope walk, trying to locate and apply to other companies, scheduling interviews in the middle of the workday, and generally trying to balance these new activities with the demands of the current job. It also becomes challenging, talking about upcoming plans and work assignments with the current boss, who at this moment is unaware of the impending departure. It can be a stressful time.

But Jellyvision's management says, "Don't worry. If you want to leave, we will make the process as comfortable for you as possible. We will give you great flexibility to schedule interviews, we will guarantee you excellent references, and your pay and benefits will stay intact until the time you officially leave." In other words, there will be no punishment for wanting to jump ship. We will try to make things a better fit for you, but if you really want to leave, we will help take the stress out of it. They call it their "graceful exit" program.

So why do you think they would do something like this? Why would a company help someone out who is clearly demonstrating that they do not want to be there?

Well, for a start, it's a nice way to behave. It's a nice way to treat a person, and as we all know, much of business is about who we know, and much of life is about how we treat people and how we make them feel. A strong, diverse network of good people who hold you in good stead is always an asset.

But more importantly, perhaps, these actions aren't just for the benefit of the person who is getting off the boat; they are for the longer-term benefit of the people who are staying on. It helps with the idea of building a connected culture, which we find at the core of *One Team, One Heart*. It shows we are together from start to finish. Kelly Dean, Jellyvision's Vice President of People, puts it this way: "Fundamentally, what drives retention here more than anything, and it's a very unconventional thing, is that we trust people and we treat them like adults. And we expect them to behave in the same way."[1]

These demonstrations of respect and cooperation will be observed and noted by the rest of the team and eventually by customers. So this offboarding process is about building and maintaining group morale through your actions, even toward a departing team member. The respect that you show to this departing individual will touch the hearts of the remaining team members much more profoundly than any motivational words ever could.

---

[1] Moran, Gwen. "These Are the Three Things to Invest in to Build Employee Loyalty." Retrieved from Fast Company online: www.fastcompany.com/40571881/these-are-the-three-things-to-invest-in-to-build-employee-loyalty

At the End of the Day, It's Not Just About the Technology

When you pick up or download a book on high-performance distributed teams, it's easy to think it's all about clear communication and project management spread over large distances. And although those components must exist here, it's also about the fact that the end points of a distributed team are all people, and they need the same types of attention and awareness as they would have if they all worked together in the same building. The good news is, despite their distance, it is easier than ever to deliver what they need.

Key Takeaways

- Being able to read the mood of a team is a vital management skill, equally applicable to distributed teams.

- Workplace is a balance between formalized activities and informal interaction. Both must exist and be supported.

- People who are part of your community will observe how others are treated. All of this will filter into morale and productivity.

Your Choice of Words Matters

There's a big difference between using buzzwords and establishing a proactive common terminology. In boating, for example, ropes are called *lines,* sails are called *sheets,* and of course the left and right sides of any vessel are referred to as *port* and *starboard*, respectively (Figure 12-1).

Many of these nautical terms have long historical and cultural roots. Starboard (originally pronounced *steer-board*) referred to the fact that the right-hand side of a vessel was where the steering oar was mounted and used (before the invention of the center-mounted rear rudder), and the left-hand side of the boat was where people could embark or disembark by way of a gangplank or steps, so this was always the side that was pulled up to the dockside, often called the port.

© Alberto S. Silveira Jr. 2021
A. S. Silveira Jr., *Building and Managing High-Performance Distributed Teams*,
https://doi.org/10.1007/978-1-4842-7055-4_12

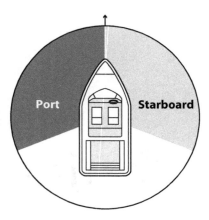

Figure 12-1. Port and starboard

The sidelights of any vessel are always red (port/left side) and green (starboard/right side) to help others determine if another vessel is approaching or traveling in the same direction. Both green and red stand out clearly against the colors of water, sky, and land in any conditions. An easy trick to remember which is which is that Port wine is red, as is the port sidelight, and "red" and "left" have the same short "e" vowel. At a fancy dinner party, a guest might ask, "Is there any red port left?"

Consistent, memorable terms of communication are vital for comprehension, and I have already mentioned the NATO alphabet in Chapter 8. This differs from buzzwords, however, in terms of the value of their meanings. Pilots and sailors take the NATO language very seriously and treat it with respect. It has a job to do, and it keeps their teams safe.

With business buzzwords, it's a sad situation when a valuable term becomes meaningless through overuse, and there are many lists online of the most hated ones. Terms like *synergy, think outside the box, take it offline,* and many, many more tend to result in eye-rolling from team members and come across as insincere. Even the term *North Star* can fall into this bucket when it gets overused without substance behind it.

These were all good terms at one time. Some words just pass out of favor as one generation replaces another. I don't hear people using the word *groovy* much anymore. Other terms, like *dude*, never seem to go out of fashion.

The point is words must stand for themselves and must deliver consistent value for members of any team. They are a crucial part of streamlined, clear communication of ideas and concepts. Very often, though, they are simply used to fill the air with sounds that make someone sound smart or well informed, when they actually are not. They are also used to add grandiosity to an otherwise insignificant term. This, again, is mere puffery.

Because we are working with people and because communication is vital to the success of any team, words become powerful tools of togetherness and motivation. Personally, I think the terms I highlighted earlier, *synergy*, *think outside the box*, and *take it offline*, are all very good terms. The problem is they have been overused, many times in the wrong context, and have lost their dignity and relevance.

When you choose terms that are going to be central to the effectiveness of your team, they must be chosen for their meaning and their value, and they must be reinforced by delivering value every time they are used. If you want to talk about *synergy*, then make sure your team knows exactly what your definition of *synergy* is and why you are using it.

In one extreme case, I learned of a company that used the word *synergy* in the context of justifying mass layoffs, as if the people being fired were voluntarily aligning themselves to its new cost-cutting plan. That, to me, is misleading and also does damage to the word for those who wish to use it for what it really is: the combining of positive forces. Leaders often shrink from the challenge of dealing with firing people and have used similar words to dull the pain of the event. Terms like rightsizing, downsizing, letting go, or making redundant all remove the human person from the situation and focus on the act itself. The person is thrown out of the transaction with the same indignity as the way they are being thrown out of their job. And the person doing the firing gets to feel less involved, both physically and emotionally.

Think about that for a moment. What does that choice of words say about the leader of that corporate team? What message does it send to the team members who remain employed? People are good at spotting fakes. Insincere and cowardly leaders are quickly outed through their words and actions. Those who remain behind and who have not been fired—as of yet—know they are working with someone who does not truly understand that the fabric of their company culture is made up entirely of people. Once they pick up on such insincerity, that fabric weakens and starts to fray on its own.

So when a manager fires someone using terms that feel comfortable to that manager by avoiding the bitterness of the act, it might seem like the problem has been solved—having got rid of a few extra people—but in truth, the real problem is just starting, as the distrust and fear foments among the rest of the staff. On a boat at sea, morale is vital. A crew working together on a vessel can easily spot a weak captain or officer. Once morale is lost, the boat starts to drift.

If you realize you have been using these terms, the reason might simply be that you have absorbed them from your surroundings as corporate slang and have not given it much thought. But now would be a good time to think about the terms you use. They are more than just words. They should always convey an awareness of and concern for the people they are being delivered to.

Sometimes terms lose their value because other people may have tainted them. *"Think outside the box"* was a good metaphor for creative thinking at one time, but when it gets used without the right context, all the magic just gets squeezed out of it. It can be the same with the term *North Star* or even *mission statement.* If everyone just nods and gives lip service to these terms without fully understanding them and being able to explain their meanings, then, yes, the terms go stale.

This is why, whenever I visit a company that I am consulting with, I always like to ask employees and executives if they know their company's mission statement by heart or if they can explain their North Star to me. If they cannot, then the term has lost its value and must be rescued.

This is also why I choose my own terms very carefully, I think about where and how to use them, and I make sure they become part of the culture in a positive way that demonstrates results and fosters additional team togetherness.

Maybe We Should Focus on Life, Not Death

Much of the traditional approach to progress has an aggressive, battle-ready, take no prisoners mindset that packages team effort into an all-or-nothing military-style advance. Often, this starts in a *war room,* which was the term used for a singular space where charts could be put up on the wall and people could make decisions. Perhaps this term was a product of its time, but equating a project to war is, I feel, counterproductive.

With the advent of the distributed teams model, we have the opportunity to focus more on *collaboration spaces* instead of *war rooms,* which I think sets a far more proactive tone for pursuing progress.

The same goes for the *postmortem.* This term is often used in business to talk about the review period after a project. It's great to have a review period, of course; in fact, it is a key component of the fifth phase of a formalized project, one governed by the rules and knowledge base of the Project Management Institute. That fifth phase is called the closure phase. It is a review period that continuous improvement comes from, and it's way better to have one than to not have one.

But I hate that term! To me a postmortem conjures up images of a dead body. It's a medical procedure designed to determine a cause of death. A project, even a completed project, is not a dead thing. It lives on through its achievements, its deliverables, and through the projects that follow it, and it supports the idea of continuous improvement.

I prefer the term *retrospective,* again not for semantic or purely grammatical reasons, but because I believe that every component that goes into building a team, especially a distributed team, must deliver positivity and inclusiveness, and I feel *retrospective* best illustrates reflecting, learning, and keeping lessons from the past alive.

Baby Steps

This is one of my favorite terms. Its origins are pretty clear. When babies first learn to walk, it's quite a magical moment. They discover a new independence that marks the beginning of a new phase of life. They cross over one of their own first equators, transitioning from a helpless infant to the beginnings of a self-aware and eventually independent person. But every baby who discovers walking soon rediscovers gravity. Their desire to walk everywhere must be tempered by the reality that walking takes practice. A baby's steps must be small and carefully thought about before they can become a larger, more confident, unconscious activity.

Baby steps are the most reliable way to climb toward the North Star.

A team-based project needs to understand the concept of baby steps, because getting to a goal of any sort requires a great deal of effort, and there will always be setbacks. One important aspect of baby steps is that each represents one step closer to the North Star. This is why I constantly use the terms *baby steps* and *continuous improvement* together. The idea is that as long as we are moving forward toward our goals while we simultaneously keep learning, that is a positive move. One step at a time, we will get to our destination. Patience is a virtue!

This is a key reality for leaders. It's nice to have a great kickoff to a project, but there will always be storms, choppy waters, or even doldrums ahead. And as I have already mentioned, the negative emotional impact that these have on team members can be stronger and longer-lasting than the positive ones.

It's vital to give people the realistic awareness that progress comes in small, measured amounts, at least at first. Look at pandemic-induced shifts to meeting by video chat, for example. Millions of people who had never participated in a company video chat prior to 2020 suddenly found themselves thrust into a new reality. It took a great deal of trial and error for individuals to learn how to set up, use, and participate in a video chat. Similarly, it is proving to be quite an experience for managers, who must learn the vital elements of distributed teams management in a hurry: how to learn, lead, and demonstrate trust via video.

This shift to working with video collaboration technology would have been a great "baby steps" project for a team, one that would have given people a chance to iteratively learn and practice the techniques of connecting and communicating in a visual space while dealing with its challenges, such as temporary disconnections or bored kids and pets joining the meeting.

I use the term *baby steps* a lot, and I try daily to make sure it does not descend into a trite cliché, by constantly seeking to deliver value and relevance each time I use it. Repetition is key, and just like learning to walk, repeated practice does indeed make perfect.

Elephant Carpaccio

Soon after mastering those "baby steps," young kids become enamored with two things: stories and large animals. They captivate our imaginations and help build an understanding of the world outside. They are also a wonderful bonding process, and the comfort that stories deliver never fades. In fact, one of the best ways to get the attention of a team of adults, whether they are sitting in front of you as a live audience or as part of a mosaic of faces in a group video chat, is to start by saying, "Let me tell you a story." When people hear that phrase, they will relax into a state of readiness that is channeled directly from their memories of early childhood.

In terms of large animals, the elephant is as large as you can get, at least on land. So it's natural that the elephant has long been used as a metaphor due to its size and strength. The most common elephant-related saying is "How do you eat an elephant? One bite at a time." This is an obvious analogy that refers to the art of breaking down a large project into manageable pieces. This, in turn, is the essence of work breakdown structure (WBS), a project management term that facilitates the planning and tracking of tasks.

On an individual level, breaking down large tasks into manageable sections goes a long way in overcoming panic, confusion, and procrastination while maximizing the skills of prioritization and time management. Fear, as we have seen in Chapter 11, is stronger than intellect and can easily lead to the breakdown of a team or a project. By illustrating a large or challenging issue as a series of small bites, especially when written out on a commonly accessible surface like a smartboard, it becomes possible to neutralize the fear with the facts.

Elephant Carpaccio is an extension of the one-bite-at-a-time metaphor and is a great tool used in incremental development. It was coined by Alistair Cockburn, a computer scientist who is best known in software and IT circles as one of the initiators of the Agile movement and was a signatory to the Manifesto for Agile Software Development.[1] This document is considered to be a classic that ushered in significant changes to the software development

---

[1] https://agilemanifesto.org/

industry and was instrumental in the creation of the DevOps movement. This is relevant to my story as a software specialist, but I hope you find it equally so, even if your industry is not IT related, because a fundamental component of Agile involves tearing down the walls and siloes of the traditional workplace and replacing them with a more dynamic and blended approach.

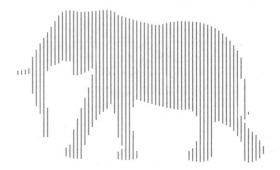

Figure 12-2. Elephant Carpaccio

Transitioning from the one-bite-at-a-time analogy to the Elephant Carpaccio analogy means placing focus on slices (Figure 12-2) rather than bites. This is not arbitrary wordplay. Elephant Carpaccio encourages people to break projects into "thin vertical slices," which Cockburn suggests are easier to implement, allowing for software products to be built and shipped in a way that delivers value in each slice and in an optimized timeframe.

When you don't have the vertical slices, you may end up having teams delivering "stuff" to end users, but that doesn't mean they are delivering actual value. The Elephant Carpaccio imagery carries with it the notion of small slices of the end product being presented in sequence, which adds even greater value. They're not just loosely lying around. The alternative of that is to have teams working on and delivering pieces that are hard to validate in terms of value until the whole elephant has been delivered, as was typical during the older, traditional Waterfall approach to software delivery that Cockburn helped change.

Equally significant here is that Elephant Carpaccio is like the opposite side of the elephant metaphor. Using the *one-bite-at-a-time* imagery usually works when you are trying to break down a large problem. Elephant Carpaccio is more about building something up iteratively. With Elephant Carpaccio, small pieces of any project can be received, understood, and used. You can then iterate and make something larger and then even larger. But you're always constantly building, delivering, and observing in a perpetual cycle, where the current cycle is always better than the previous one.

The Deming Cycle and Continuous Improvement

The concepts of baby steps and Elephant Carpaccio blend very well into the philosophies of continuous improvement that I have described a couple of times already, especially with regard to Lean management, Agile, *gemba* walks, and *kaizen*.

As a team, we are always on a voyage. No organization can ever simply hold still and define their current situation as the new normal or the new status quo. Holding still is like treading water when swimming in the ocean or bringing your boat to a stop without dropping anchor. You might no longer be using energy to move, but the forces around you will move you anyway, and usually that's not a good thing. In business, holding onto a norm, to a status quo, inevitably leads to decline. Innovation and constant forward motion are required—at the very minimum to stay in one place, but even more importantly to keep moving forward against the relentless forces of progress and change.

Some of the productivity concepts for distributed team members that I have already described—like Focus Time, Catch-up Time, Collaboration Time blocking, and the use of synchronous and asynchronous communication—must all be reviewed, improved, and practiced regularly, not only to ensure that they are being used correctly but to address the fact that they all have to be used on a platform that is continuously moving and changing. In the companies I have worked for and the training sessions I have delivered, I would repeat these techniques many times, even after we as a group had created and agreed upon them, because none of this is happening in a static environment.

Even before the pandemic, the business world was changing, and people were investigating variations of the distributed teams model and the use of collaboration technology. Change continues to happen, and the pace of change tends to keep increasing. The year 2020 forced this into overdrive, but it was happening anyway. So making baby steps toward a goal of continuous improvement should not be seen as a pairing of clichés. It's a mission statement that establishes a company's goals and focuses people's energies and talents.

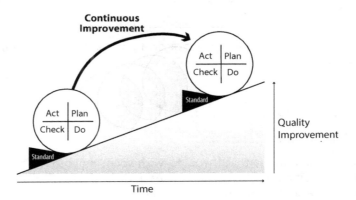

Figure 12-3. Continuous improvement

This is where the Deming Cycle (Figure 12-3) comes in. It is one of those concepts that withstand the test of time due to their sheer simplicity. It is a practical application of continuous improvement and the "baby steps" approach that is easy to explain and therefore easy to universally understand.

The Deming Cycle dates back to 1959 and was part of the Toyota Production Management (TPM) business process that forms much of the project management approach that we use to this day. The cycle refers to the fact that the process is cyclical. It consists of four actions: plan, do, check, adjust, sometimes written as plan, do, check, act. Every process must be planned first, then run, then reviewed to check against calculations and expectations, and then improved and adjusted accordingly. This is why it is fundamental to the entire concept of continuous improvement.

This image of the Deming Cycle drives home the idea of continuous improvement by envisioning the plan-do-check-adjust concepts like a round boulder being rolled uphill. Each time you complete a full rotation of plan-do-check-adjust, you jam a wedge under the boulder to stop it rolling backward. That wedge represents the new standard, the new *normal for now*. That's what continuous improvement is all about.

We need to jam that wedge in and define a new normal, not just because it's nice to do but because circumstances demand it. For an individual person, it might start when a person is onboarded, and it must continue from there. For teams, it starts with the formation of the team. In both cases, we must add and test new skills and identify and then eliminate wasteful or counterproductive ones. Practices that work well must be spotlighted, revised, and reinforced. It's not just up to the captain; it is the job of every team member or crew member to keep repeating the message and grow it within the team, no matter where each member lives and works.

It is not just up to the captain. Every crew member must grow the message within the team.

The Need to Write It All Down and Synthesize

One of the organizations that I worked with spent much of its time focusing on objectives, using the OKRs (Objectives and Key Results) model. Through this, they believed they had the type of measurable company objective that they had always wanted. The problem was, although they were using this objective companywide, it was not written anywhere concisely.

When I started working with them, senior management was intrigued by how much writing I did. They admitted to me that they didn't have a culture of writing. I responded to the leadership team by saying, "If we don't write it down, it doesn't exist." I went on to explain that when ideas, definitions, standards, and procedures are not written, people will rely on their own subjective interpretations, and that can lead to confusion and inefficiency.

Committing ideas to a tangible surface like paper or a smartboard not only becomes a place of record, it also allows people to start down a creative path that comes from reading those notes and letting the mind do what it does best. By contrast, any person or organization that shies away from the effort of writing is condemning people to stick with only those initial thoughts and is allowing no room for expansion of those thoughts.

This particular company felt it was doing well. Its teams had high-level areas of focus. They had projects. They had good people and everyone was busy. Those people were working on "stuff" that in theory supported their objectives. I suggested to them that having people working on "stuff" is good, but if you, and they, cannot answer the following three basic questions, then it will not be possible to confirm that all of their "stuff" was actually moving the boat forward toward the North Star. The three questions are

1. What is our goal?

2. What problem are we trying to solve?

3. How are we going to be measuring success?

If they cannot answer those three basic questions for every project, they should really think about analyzing how they are investing their time. Once the team can answer these three questions consistently and as a team, that's when they can start to slice the answers into smaller pieces, Elephant Carpaccio–style. Every component that is created, whether it is a widget or code, must be designed with the end user or customer in mind. It should become almost an obsession. It should also be manageable and verifiable.

I implemented Elephant Carpaccio at this company, and it wasn't long before it became central to all the planning sessions they held, day to day, from that point on. Most significantly, the C-level leadership team started talking about it, which went a long way toward ensuring everybody else did.

The Elephant Carpaccio exercise also introduced them to the concept of the Iron Triangle and helped them visualize the priorities of their three key groups: engineering was always thinking about the technology, the product people were always thinking about the market and how they were going to close the competitive gaps, and the product designers were always thinking about the user experience. By applying the Iron Triangle, they were able to rein in and balance these priorities while simultaneously breaking down their internal silos and replacing them with a flatter, more accessible culture.

In this company, as in others I have worked with, one of the answers that I had to give quite often when speaking to its leader, to the board of investors, or to the people from marketing, sales, and other areas was that they should not only be able to slice the metaphorical elephant in terms of building their projects, but they should also be able to identify where they are investing their efforts and energies the most.

I encouraged them to look at each part of the triangle to see where the company was building more features, scaling up infrastructure or security, or adding more issues around user experience. I drove home the importance of slicing these up, Carpaccio-style, to understand and prioritize their investments in energy, people, and resources. All of that without losing the focus on the North Star.

This is all achievable once we have established and documented terminologies, processes, project standards, and decisions along the journey. At the end of the day, if we don't write it down, it doesn't exist, at least not in a consistent, repeatable, and measurable way.

Policies, Guidelines, and Rules! Oh My!

I am also careful to distinguish between my choice of words and actions around procedure. One example I can provide from my past is around the word *diversity*. I was working as part of a company's executive team when, during a meeting, one employee asked what we were doing for diversity. I had to ask myself what that term meant in relation to the company itself. It might appear obvious at first glance, but this is a word that has many layers.

We discovered that we did not have a clear definition for *diversity*, and so we did not have clear actions and metrics to support it. We immediately created a committee open to any employees to join, and we quickly made progress. We were able to come up with a proper definition of what diversity meant for us and what the actions should be, and we also implemented the appropriate initiatives and plans.

I often get inquiries from people asking how my teams were able to achieve what they did and what policies were put in place to make this happen. The first thing I tell them is it's not just about policies; success centers around a balanced collection of rules, policies, guidelines, procedures, and standards, which vary in their levels of personal accountability. A clearly designed, well-maintained collection of these items offers a much more solid plan for high-performance team dynamics and continuous improvement.

Rules

I am not fond of hard rules generally, since they can inhibit creativity and initiative when applied to the wrong areas. However, in terms of supporting a team and its activities, I do agree that it is vital to implement and share some clear and consistent rules to avoid getting into a situation in which one person says "A" and the other hears or interprets it as "B."

For example, organizations really should enforce two-factor or multifactor authentication (2FA/MFA) to enhance endpoint security. Currently, 2FA/MFA is a policy, but I feel it should be a rule, the same way that boats and planes must follow the globally enforced rules of identification such as using red and green lights to identify the port and starboard sides of a vessel. You must not do it the other way around or choose different colored lights. Rules must be rigid and inflexible and must be applied in the right circumstances in scenarios that need no room for personal interpretation.

Policies

Policies guide decision-making but leave some room for individual choice. For example, a dress code policy in the workplace ensures a degree of appropriateness while not thwarting personal preferences.

Policies can be strict. They are often formal statements produced and supported by senior management in the organization. Maternity leave is a policy. The open door policy ensures employees have access to their managers and conversely that managers cannot seal themselves away through meetings and tightly blocked schedules. Data replication policy may speak to how data may be copied. Where that copied data can be stored might be a policy or a rule, depending on data privacy legislation such as HIPAA and GDPR. Work from anywhere can be a policy, as can "if you see something, say something" promoted by the New York City Transit Authority (Chapter 9).

Guidelines

Guidelines give direction but allow for the widest range of interpretation, generally in support of an objective. They are intended to empower people to collaborate and make things better, using their own initiative, but within established parameters.

The *dotted lines* concept that I described in Chapter 9 reflects this. Similarly, my suggestions of using message prefixes in email subject lines for clearer communication (also Chapter 8) and scheduling *retrospectives* after an event are all examples of guidelines. I could have made them compulsory activities, in other words rules, but I would rather leave this type of decision-making up to each team or individual.

Procedures

You could think of rules as a must-do, while guidelines are something a person might want to do, but a procedure is definitely a how to do. A procedure includes detailed step-by-step instructions to achieve a given goal. Examples in the workplace could include how to report time off, how to set up a VPN, how to submit an expense report, how to release a new version of an application, how to report a bug in the system, or how to exit a building safely upon hearing the fire alarm. Each of these involves a number of steps that should be followed.

Standards

A standard is a repeatable, reliable, agreed-upon, and documented way of achieving something. Standards contain some sort of technical specifications or other precise criteria designed to be used consistently and efficiently throughout a process such as product development.

Another way to look at this is to compare it to a rule. A rule describes an action before it happens. You might say, "Every boat entering or leaving a harbor must proceed at dead slow, leaving no wake." A standard establishes the consistent and exact criteria of that rule—it is the reason for the rule's existence and offers an opportunity for retrospective and analysis, as in "Did we meet the standard today? Did all boats travel dead slow? How many offenses were observed?"

Examples in the workplace could include naming convention standards, database creation standards, and observability standards. Standards can still have a dotted lines component in the sense that an individual is empowered to act in a way that will meet them, but overall, the team agrees to, or is required to, follow those standards more rigorously.

As you can see, there is great potential for overlap between these concepts, depending on how tightly they are defined and how much leeway individuals are given in following them. But just like my discussion of the NATO alphabet and Seaspeak in Chapter 8, the importance of an agreed-upon and universally understood culture within a team, whether distributed or on-premises, is what is most important. Ambiguity and uncertainty must be eliminated. All communication, collaboration, and future success depends on this.

Setting Clear Expectations: The Career Ladder

For teams and team members, setting clear expectations is key. Obviously, the words chosen to describe roles and responsibilities are vital. I have used this as part of a career ladder, which in my past company we described as follows:

> *A competency career ladder is the combination of observable and measurable knowledge, skills, abilities, and personal attributes that contribute to enhanced employee performance, and ultimately result in organizational success.*[2]

Throughout my career, as I have stated, I have worked for numerous companies spanning different industries, and I have seen and experienced some long, complex, and hard-to-understand career ladders. When these career ladders become difficult, people tend to ignore them. This means the expectations set for each role and level are seldom met and people feel less able to improve and move ahead. The lack of clarity frustrates them.

Managers find that they, too, are unable to guide their team members consistently, which causes further misalignment and an unbalanced environment. All of these failings ultimately lead to a team going offtrack and missing its connection to its North Star.

The reason career ladders are important is so that people have—and can see—the clear path of their own journey within their careers—their own personal North Star. The same thing applies to crew members in a boat: it is important to have a list of competencies and expectations. From the entry level to the most senior rank on board (usually captain), the set of competencies might be the same, but the expectations for each level will be different and more comprehensive.

---

[2]Retrieved from www.researchgate.net/publication/292308102_Employee_Core_Competencies_for_Effective_Talent_Management

I have built successful ladders with my teams by making them simple through the principle of "less is more." To that end, I always seek to use fewer words.

I like to set clear expectations for each competency per role level. This to me is a far better type of scorecard—one that allows for continuous checking and continuous improvement, rather than relying on the outdated concept of annual performance review. As you can see, this has parallels to continuous testing in DevOps. If I cannot explain a job or a task in a single sentence, I feel it means I do not fully understand it. So how can I expect a team member to do any better? In the end, the choice of words does matter.

Key Takeaways

- Terms and words have a great impact on a team's sense of progress and destiny.

- Concepts like continuous improvement and Elephant Carpaccio are used frequently in team discussions because they have been proven to work.

- Using fewer words, avoiding buzzwords, and giving credence to the terminologies you adapt will be noted by your team members and will form part of their team culture.

The Power of Repetition

It is extremely important to factor in repetition to a culture; in fact, you really can't have one without the other. It is the recurrence of activities, words, and principles that forms a culture. Humans crave regularity and consistency. These elements reinforce people's sense of safety by staying as a known commodity, and they strengthen social bonds.

For centuries people have convened for all types of ceremonies and events: religious services, weddings, national and local holidays, Sunday Night Football, sailing regattas, and so on. The list of regular, consistent activities is endless and is central to all cultures of the world. The year 2020 showed just how vital such activities are to people, especially in regard to the thousands of examples in which people defied isolation requests in order to continue their get-togethers.

Some of the repetitive elements of an on-premises workplace tend to get overlooked, because their regularity becomes part of the background. The commute to work, for example, and the activities of the workplace—meetings, coffee breaks, using the elevators—may seem like humdrum day-to-day elements of the workday, but they remain reassuring in their repetitiveness. People might look forward to Friday, the end of the week for many, but deep

© Alberto S. Silveira Jr. 2021
A. S. Silveira Jr., *Building and Managing High-Performance Distributed Teams*,
https://doi.org/10.1007/978-1-4842-7055-4_13

down, the awareness that there will be another week to come gives most people an instinctive sense of comfort.

Obviously, distributed teams do not have the commute and the office space, by definition. But repetition of actions and principles remains vital and very attainable. As a leader of a distributed team, it is your job to determine the amount of repetition needed to build and strengthen the team.

Some of these may be calendar related such as

- Scheduling a team huddle via video chat at a regular day and time, such as 11:00 a.m. every Monday

- Ensuring team members' regular accessibility to you through a flexible online shared calendar

Some may be consistency related such as

- Establishing a regular pattern of referring to the North Star and soliciting feedback from individuals

- Ensuring your style of video chat meeting, both for groups and one-on-ones, remains consistent in style and possibly duration

- Using email subject line prefixes and other forms of standardized communication as described in Chapter 8

- Maintaining a regular MBWA/gemba habit as described in Chapter 11

Some may be social, such as

- Making time and budget available for social online get-togethers

- Ensuring regular physical get-togethers at least once per year

The point here is that repetition is like mortar or cement in that it holds all the components of a structure together. In this case, the structure is the team of people distributed geographically. It is easy to think that it is the Internet connection that brings a distributed team together, but, no, that's just a tool—a vital one, but a tool all the same. It is consistency of word and action, the product of repetition, and a clear understanding of the needs of the "working human" that has always been the success factor of any group undertaking. It aligns with people's tribal instincts in exactly the same way the rhythms of music align with the human heartbeat.

A friend of mine once paraphrased David Gergen, saying on the subject of repetition, "If you want to get your point across, especially to a broader audience, you need to repeat yourself so often, you get sick of hearing yourself say it. And only then will people begin to internalize what you're saying…When you are tired of saying it, people are starting to hear it."

—Jeff Weiner, former CEO of LinkedIn (2009–2020), now Executive Chairman[1]

Repetition Is Key to Learning

On a more physical level, repetition is used to assist with learning and to develop effective work habits. It is key to converting information into knowledge. As anyone who has ever crammed for an exam knows, most new information does not stick on the first go-around.

There are four types of memory that can be factored into a team: long-term memory, short-term memory, muscle memory, and collective team culture. Here's why—and how—each is central to building and maintaining a distributed teams culture.

1. Long-term memory: How to learn more effectively

Long-term memory is where knowledge and experiences go and remain stored for most of a person's life. There is no one single area of the brain where memories are stored. Much like a cluttered house, memories can be stored all over the place.

The general understanding is that they are coordinated by the hippocampus, which sits in the center. Profoundly significant events and emotionally powerful events need only to be experienced once to be indelibly printed into long-term memory. Think about the birth of a child into your family or a bad experience like an accident, a disaster-type event, or news of the death of a famous person. These types of memories tend to get flash frozen because of their dense emotional impact.

But when it comes to working with teams, there is always a need to teach team members new skills and knowledge. But this will not happen instantly because most of what people learn professionally is not emotionally shocking in nature.

---

[1]Retrieved from GetLightHouse.com. https://getlighthouse.com/blog/power-of-repetition-successful-leaders/

Learning and eventual mastery come from the desire to develop better skills through knowledge, and for knowledge to happen, people need effective teaching methods. For decades in the workplace scenario, managers have sent employees to training sessions, where they would sit all day in a classroom and try to learn what was shown.

Why were they sent to a classroom? Because that's how we all experienced learning from kindergarten through to college or university. Almost all of it was done in class, in a formalized, modularized, and impersonal way. But this was never an ideal learning method for most students, whether in school or in a corporate training session. Why? Because people can't learn and retain eight hours' worth of new information unless they do something practical that will massage it into their minds and muscles. Short-term teaching just cannot do that alone. Even in the best of immersive and interactive situations, there is still only a fixed amount that can be absorbed before people move into information overload.

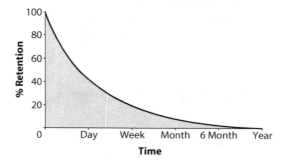

Figure 13-1. Ebbinghaus Forgetting Curve

Figure 13-1 is the Ebbinghaus Forgetting Curve, which is based on a mathematical formula devised by German psychologist Hermann Ebbinghaus in 1885. That's a long time ago, but it doesn't matter, because even though technology has changed enormously over the past century and a half, human beings have not changed that much physically or mentally. We still have the same capacity to learn or forget as our great-great-grandparents did.

The main impact of this image curve is to show the rate at which information is forgotten when people are not given the opportunity to practice it to the ultimate level of near perfection.

This means that if I were to deliver a class—in a room or online—for a full day, the students would be lucky if, just 24 hours later, they could remember 40 percent of what I said. A week later, that retention rate will be halved again to 20 percent. This type of education has never been a great investment in anyone's time.

But with the distributed teams model, we have the opportunity to reconstruct learning along more human lines. We no longer need to cram people into a room to hear the same message at the same time over a scant few hours, sharing the very limited resources of a single instructor among the entire group.

Online education is an industry I know very well. Consequently, I know first-hand there are far more effective ways of imparting skills and knowledge to individual students, using the same technologies that hold distributed teams together: video, media, and the Internet.

Teaching can and should be divided into smaller micro-modules, accessible according to individual students' own schedules and necessity and learning abilities and enhanced through augmented reality, virtual reality, artificial intelligence, and machine learning. This will help structure dynamic teaching methods that address an individual student's strengths and weaknesses and that identify those weak areas for review and additional focus. This technology allows information to be prioritized to meet people's needs rather than the needs of the educational institution.

But most importantly, repetition is key to learning. When this is paired with more customized learning opportunities, distributed team members will generate and reinforce the habits and knowledge that are vital for working together and of course for producing a viable end product.

This means budgeting the time and the resources for a more repetitive and modular style of teaching, far removed from day-long lectures and focused on more iterative baby steps toward skills and knowledge development.

2. Short-term memory: How to think creatively

Human short-term memory is like the RAM (random access memory) of a computer—it's the moment-by-moment processing of thoughts and stimuli, much of which gets forgotten very quickly.

The problem is we humans don't have very much of it. People can generally hold only about eight items in short-term memory at a time. This is a concept that has been understood since the 1950s when George Miller of Harvard University's Department of Psychology published a work that eventually was referred to as Miller's Law.[2] That's why it's so easy to lose your train of thought when you get distracted—the distraction bumps one of those eight items out of the way. I like to think of it like a juggler who can juggle eight balls or clubs at a time, but no more.

---

[2]The work is entitled "The Magical Number Seven, Plus or Minus Two: Some Limits on Our Capacity for Processing Information." *Psychological Review.* 63 (2): 81–97. It is one of many works that support the concept of short-term or "primary" memory.

From a distributed teams perspective, this apparent weakness in human thinking actually has an enormous strength in the form of a single, simple tool—the online smartboard.

When people use smartboards or even pen, paper, and easels to move preliminary ideas out of short-term memory and store them safely on that surface, it frees up space in short-term memory for new ideas to pour in. To go back to the juggler analogy, by throwing one ball or bowling pin away, the juggler now has the ability to accept and integrate a new one. That's how creative thinking and brainstorming work. You have to let go of something that is being held in short-term memory in order for a new idea to germinate. The online smartboard is perfect for that. (Note that the smartboard is just an example. There are many collaboration tools available these days that can achieve the same.)

Furthermore, placing ideas onto a smartboard surface simultaneously allows other team members to see those same ideas at the same time, and when this happens, the team benefits from a group creativity session that tends to exceed the sum of the parts. This is what synergy actually involves.

Of course, this technique can be used in an on-premises office situation as well—the dry-erase board and the paper easel have done wonders for meeting room brainstorming sessions for decades. But distributed teams are in an ideal place to capitalize on both the creative thinking and synergy opportunities that smartboards provide as well as the convenience of not needing to travel to a specific room to do it.

3. Muscle memory: How to act efficiently

Muscle memory is sometimes called force of habit. For example, if you store your breakfast coffee mug in a particular cupboard in your kitchen, you will inevitably reach for it without thinking each time you make yourself a coffee. Muscle memory comes from repeated physical action and usually takes around 20 days of conscious repetition before it gets absorbed into the body. Once there, it no longer requires conscious remembering—the body and the muscles take over and do things automatically.

There are plenty of ways in which muscle memory can be used. For distributed teams, probably the best and most productive example is to train team members to do one thing at a time and focus on the conversation that is happening. People compulsively multitask, feeling a need to check emails or even scroll through a web page while having a conversation. Although this may be a result of personality or short attention span, a far better way for team members to collaborate is to generate and reinforce the capacity to focus on one task at a time.

In truth, when people work on numerous things simultaneously, they are not truly multitasking so much as "fast switching" their attention between numerous activities. This is never as productive as total focus. Training a person to resist the temptation to multitask becomes an act of physical muscle memory reprogramming. It really helps when, first, the team culture supports a policy of focus in place of multitasking—this delivers social permission and acceptance. Then the activity of changing one's habits and reflexes away from multitasking becomes a muscle memory exercise.

A second and more direct example of muscle memory is to teach team members to hesitate before clicking email or text message links. Phishing and similar cybercrimes are getting more sophisticated by the day, but most still rely on an unwitting individual clicking a link, especially when they are distracted by a message such as "your bank account has been frozen" or "my job application is attached." Many people already know that clicking phishing links allows malware to be injected into a computer and then propagate through every other connected computer, but that still doesn't stop people from clicking them.

This is a concept that applies equally to distributed teams as to on-premises teams. Its importance rests in training the body and mind to overrule that moment of desire to click the link in a message and replace it with a pause long enough for second-guessing. As simple as it seems, successful deployment of this muscle memory technique can save endless amounts of trouble and damage.

4. Team memory: How to grow collectively

Team memory is the fourth of these memory types and can be thought of also as a collective team culture that pulls these new habits together. It involves the techniques of long-term, short-term, and muscle memory, but what is most important here is that once established, the culture is encouraged to evolve and continuously improve, reinforced through proactive, team-oriented activities like the huddles and social events I described earlier. Case studies like Netflix (Chapter 9) and the companies that appear in those best places to work lists show that team memory and collective team culture are self-reinforcing concepts, a positive cultural Deming Cycle.

Milestones

Milestones are tools of repetition, even if they don't look that way at first glance. Most people see them as markers along a path—something that represents an achievement or the completion of one part of a project. On an ocean excursion or cruise, ports of call could be considered milestones within the overall voyage. But milestones also serve a purpose of repetition.

Arriving at a milestone gives team members and leaders the opportunity to pause, assess the achievements of the project thus far, look ahead to what tasks remain, rest, replan, and reevaluate. This might also include maintenance and adjustment of priorities or of the team's structure. My point is a milestone is not just a marker that you simply speed past on the way to the finish line, it's a necessary opportunity to reevaluate and review and as such becomes a strategic type of repetition.

Out on the water, if crews don't take the time to repeatedly reevaluate the condition of the vessel, its equipment, and its crew and check navigation calculations, they might find themselves in a place that is quite different from where they wanted to be. That is why repetition is as much a valued component of ocean travel as are streamlined communication processes like Seaspeak.

With projects and teams, it becomes easy for people to drift away from the North Star, especially over time. Milestones are one way to revisit and repeat the objectives and the mission of the voyage and to ensure that everyone involved is still on board.

Missing Milestones at Sea: Two Tragedies a Century Apart

The history of sea travel is littered with stories of failure and tragedy, many of which can be directly related to a single event like a storm. But the resultant loss of life has much more to do with the suppression of project management habits like repetition and milestones.

Everyone knows that the cause of one of the most famous maritime tragedies, the sinking of the Titanic, was an iceberg. But the reason the boat actually collided with the iceberg, in a part of the North Atlantic where icebergs were common and expected, had more to do with procedures that were not followed correctly and milestones that were not observed. These included improper training of a crew that had been hastily assembled, including its captain, as well as inadequate repetitive practice with safety equipment including lifeboat drills, radio communication, and iceberg lookouts. These items were not practiced often enough and were not given the priority they deserved.

The stakeholders of the White Star Line, which owned the Titanic, had lost sight of their North Star, which was to "provide steady and comfortable passages for both upper class travelers and immigrants," sacrificing milestones and repetition of crucial safety elements in a rush to get to New York and show off a successful maiden voyage.

A similar thing happened a century later, when the Costa Concordia struck submerged rocks off Isola del Giglio, Italy, and came to rest at a dramatic

45-degree angle, photos of which captivated the world in 2012. This tragedy, too, was exacerbated by under-practiced safety activities. There was communication chaos, crews were unfamiliar with the safety drills, safety equipment—including lifeboats—went undertested and actually failed, and there was a complete lack of contingencies and safety procedures, which left passengers confused and terrified. Thirty-two people died.

History is filled with similar types of corporate failure too, often blamed on a single large event, but behind the scenes there is often a trail of neglect, in which the repetitive nature of milestones was overlooked or ignored out of reluctance or ignorance.

This is why milestones are so vital. They are not just about physical coordinates on a road or on a project plan. They represent opportunities to think, review, and adjust as necessary. Some of the questions you may want to ask along the journey of any project are as follows: Where is our team or company investing its time and resources, and is this still wise? How much is being invested in innovation vs. maintenance of the product? Do these decisions still correlate to current market conditions? What is happening in the marketplace right now and in the near future? Are time and resources still being invested in the most important things? Are the measurements and metrics of success still aligned with our current trajectory?

Milestones on a Shared Screen

In earlier centuries, actual milestones were road markers—stones set into the ground that told a traveler how many miles it was to the next town or castle. These stones were pretty much the only technology around for helping someone gauge how far they were from their destination or even that they were on the right path.

Today, we need to dispense with the idea that a project milestone is a marker that should be driven by at speed, on our singular quest to arrive at the target destination on time. It shouldn't exist simply in that one singular vector. As I mentioned earlier, your milestones should be a place to stop and look around, to take stock, and to question whether this most recent step forward is actually helping, whether you still want to travel toward that destination, and whether anything has changed in the interim and what else can be added to the knowledge base that we did not have at the previous milestone. They are a tool for repetitive planning and continuous improvement.

For distributed teams, milestones should be clearly identified on a visual live project map. Team members need to see the project or calendar, along with the milestones that dot the route. These data points should be front and center in every team's online knowledge platform. Having these live documents is key because they allow teams to constantly review, evaluate, and adjust the route as they move toward their North Star.

The technology that brings distributed teams together is perfect for this. Distributed team members are going to find a centralized, online document far more accessible and up-to-date than they would a binder on a shelf back at the office.

The bottom line is this: defining milestones is necessary to validate the trajectory along the journey. Repeatedly referring to them allows team members the opportunity to adjust their actions to ensure they continue to travel toward the desired destination. Milestones in a project are analogous to checkpoints at different ports in a multiday regatta. It is very unlikely that the initial coordinates will remain the same throughout an entire journey. Teams learn as they go and plans inevitably need revising.

Knots!

The ropes you use on a boat aren't called ropes; they're called "lines." When you use lines to attach a boat to the dock or to fly sails properly, you have to know which knots to use. Sometimes they are actually called knots, but other times they are called hitches, depending on what their purpose is. And there are quite a few of them. Different knots work in different ways. Some will hold fast to objects or to other ropes, while others are designed to slip on purpose. And knots should also be able to be undone quickly. Ropes that have tangles and knots in them are useless, messy, and dangerous.

The people who teach you how to tie knots and hitches will want you to practice them over and over and over again, until you can do them with your eyes closed or almost in your sleep. It's vitally important to the safety of the boat and its passengers that the right knot is used for the right purpose and that it is tied correctly. If not, your boat might slip from its moorings, your sail might fly away, or, in a worst-case scenario, a person you are trying to save from the waters may not survive.

Once you have learned your knots and hitches, you must expect to keep practicing them, as well as all the other activities involved in boating, because when people don't practice, they get rusty and that's when mistakes are made. It's the same with teams. Repetition is key.

Overcommunication Is Actually Good

There's a difference between overcommunication and excess communication. It comes down to how much is actually needed. Overcommunication is good. Redundancy can also be good. Excess usually leads to waste.

On the bridge of a large ship, the captain will regularly send commands to the engine room, the navigator, and/or the helm, regarding steering the ship or changing its speed. The standard practice for centuries has been for the command to be repeated exactly as heard. If the captain says, "All ahead full," the command is repeated exactly by an officer on the bridge, who then relays it to the engine room. The engine room says it back.

The justification for such overcommunication is likely obvious. It confirms that everyone heard the command exactly, which is far better than having the engine room say, "Yeah, OK." Pilots, too, will repeat the commands given to them from air traffic control to confirm they understand which altitude to fly, which maneuver to make, and which runway to land on.

Operating room nurses take special courses to become certified to work in an OR. One of the many things they learn there is how to hand a surgical tool to a surgeon. The surgeon does not have time to look into their own hand to ensure the correct tool is there. They rely on the OR nurse to hand it over properly, repeating the name of the tool audibly while placing the tool in the surgeon's hand with a practiced amount of pressure and technique. All of this is done as a streamlined communication technique that involves repetition, designed for a literal life-or-death situation.

Overcommunication ensures clarity and effectiveness. Excess just muddies things up. If I have a conversation with someone and they use my name at the start of every single sentence—"Alberto this... Alberto that..."—it becomes distracting and disturbing. I am likely to start to infer that this person is excessively nervous or has something to hide or, worse, is trying to sell me something.

But overcommunication can be strategic and useful in distributed team communication. It delivers consistency and clarity. I make a point to ensure that every message I create and send will use the terminologies we have agreed to, and every time I sign off, I will use the same style of signature. I make a point in my emails, text messages, and spoken words to introduce a concept, describe the concept, and then conclude by summing up the concept. This needs to be done, in text and out loud, in order to capture the minds and memories of team members.

One of the central pillars of my distributed teams strategy is *One Team, One Heart*. I have described it a couple of times already. But how do I reinforce it with my teams? How do I imprint it into that fourth level of memory—*collective team culture*? Through repetition of word and action.

When the finance team comes to say "thank you" for a great and successful monthly review meeting—one that helped us confirm that we are on track with our expenses for the month—I say back, "No problem, it's One Team, One Heart, and One Wallet." Through these words I remind the finance team, as well as everyone else, that at the end of the day, we are all in the same boat and keeping our finances aligned is vital to our voyage.

One Team. One Heart. One Wallet.

I use variations on the One Team, One Heart mantra, but they are all designed to circle back to the main concept. I might talk about "One Team, One Heart, One Shared Goal" when I am involved in planning sessions or even "One Team, One Heart, One Stomach" when we discuss the important notion of empowering distributed team members to expense their meals to ensure everyone is having a good time while meeting with the team, just as if we had walked from the office to a nearby restaurant to have lunch together.

Repetition can be enjoyable in this way, helping people live and breathe the One Team, One Heart philosophy and also helping them to reinforce its vital connection. It builds respect for each other and delivers that shared energy needed to keep moving forward.

Overcommunication Helps in Calendaring Too

When people work in distributed teams, they are obviously not in physical proximity to each other as they would be in an office. So just like the airline pilot and the OR nurse, it's a good idea to overcommunicate certain messages in order to ensure they are received and understood.

For example, a quick message sent via Slack or Microsoft Teams might not be seen among the flurry of other messages. Although I describe how to improve this in Chapter 8, the reality is not everyone may have got to that point yet. Perhaps you have agreed to a video chat meeting on Thursday at 2:00. Did everybody get that message? If they are in different time zones, do they all understand which time zone 2:00 refers to?

As simple as this point may be, it is a great practice to follow up an agreement with a shared calendar invite that includes the log-on information for the video chat and, as well, a reminder 24 hours prior or on the morning of that same day. This is not excessive overcommunication. It's the proper kind of overcommunication that we want team members to practice. It helps avoid small problems, because small problems have a tendency to grow into larger ones.

Last but not least, I really love when team members proactively share their progress on whatever they are doing. This could be simply a comment to the team room or ticket system used to track projects, such as "Today I worked on task ABCD and made near to 75 percent progress toward completion. I will continue on it tomorrow and I have no blockers."

I call this technique a "midday check-in," which is done asynchronously so other teammates know what is going on without needing to meet about it. This is similar to the more traditional early morning standup that is common on agile teams in software development, but my midday check-in is an overcommunication technique designed to ensure team members are aligned and constantly helping each other. That's the One Team, One Heart spirit in action.

Repetition is vitally important. In addition to everything I have just mentioned, it also delivers consistency of experience, which is vital to gaining people's trust and cooperation. Consistency gives people a sense of regularity, which instinctively and emotionally is far more attractive than constant change.

As we have seen, people fear the unknown, and constant change represents the unknown in a big way. That's why public figures, especially in politics and business, will choose a certain visual style and will then stick with it, with very little change, throughout their political careers, especially their choice of clothing and hairstyle. These items will remain strictly consistent throughout their tenure, because they, more so than any words spoken, are what connect with a person's instincts.

Consistency. Repetition. Reinforcement. These are concepts that speak to the human being through intellect, emotion, rhythm, and experience. They do not need to be discarded once teams become distributed; in fact, they become the mortar of their new virtual workplace.

Consistency, repetition, and reinforcement: concepts that speak to the human being through intellect, emotion, rhythm, and experience.

Key Takeaways

- Repetition is key to developing the four types of memory used by teams: long-term, short term, muscle, and team memory.

- Milestones are more than points along a path—they are opportunities for reflection and repetition.

- Overcommunication is a vital way of ensuring that even the simplest of messages get read and understood by team members.

Developing a Continuous Mindset

Many managers and productivity experts like to use the term *best practices* to describe an ideal that people should aspire to. I understand the spirit behind that term, but I personally don't like to use it with my teams because it's not *continuous* enough.

I was taught long ago that the concept of *best practices* can have two meanings. Although it is intended to represent an ongoing pursuit of continuous improvement, for many people it instead represents a fixed point in time or the attainment of a defined goal. Once people have attained that goal, they will celebrate a win. OK, that's good, but it usually means that they will then try to stick to it (that's a best-case scenario) or will drift back into the habits they had before (that's what usually happens when there is no repetition of the training). Either way, a team is doomed to slide backward toward mediocrity or failure as soon as it has stopped trying to keep pace with the perpetual change that surrounds it.

© Alberto S. Silveira Jr. 2021
A. S. Silveira Jr., *Building and Managing High-Performance Distributed Teams*,
https://doi.org/10.1007/978-1-4842-7055-4_14

The term *best practices* has some value, certainly. It's good for any company to strive to improve in order to attain the goals that they identify as a *best practice*, but the point is they must also recognize that the finish line will always keep moving forward and so teams must keep moving forward too.

To me, the concept behind *continuous improvement* is far more beneficial than a one-time improvement implied by *best practices*. Continuous always beats finite.

Continuous always beats finite.

Moving from Continuous Improvement to a Continuous Mindset

I have already mentioned how the 2020 pandemic forced teams and companies to switch to online using video chat technologies that in many cases had not been fully thought through. Once management recognized that every staff member did indeed have a laptop with a camera and high-speed Internet access, it became the new normal for meetings and work schedules to carry on as they had prior to the lockdown.

The worst examples of this were multi-hour video chat calls combined with a reluctance to recognize (a) just how different work from home really is and (b) that it is still possible to attain work objectives from this new normal. The gap was in the inability to continuously improve.

As technologies evolve, so too do people's skills, attitudes, and standards. This was true before the pandemic and will remain so long afterward. Perhaps one of the great lessons that can be learned from the work from home imperative is that organizations and teams must redesign, test, and improve their techniques repetitively. That is the essence of continuous improvement, built into the kaizen movement and the Deming Cycle as described in Chapter 12, but it needs to move beyond a process. It needs to become a mindset.

Becoming Continuous

In the earlier decades of software code writing, there were distinct groups of engineers: those who wrote the code and those who tested it for accuracy. The product cascaded down from one department to another, pouring over walls like some type of waterfall. That's what they actually called it—Waterfall.

But quickly evolving developments in the software industry, including the increased pace of new practices and technologies, led to an urgent need to consolidate and blend skill sets, just to keep up.

Consumers have no patience for websites that load slowly or apps that fail to work immediately upon download. Computers, smartphones, and machines cannot go out into the real world with bugs in their software. All code has to be heavily tested first, but the pace of the marketplace means that testing now has to happen while the product is being built. The separate worlds of software design and testing had to merge and become one continuous system, with testing shifted "left," chronologically sooner up the design process from its traditional place at its end.

The design and testing teams had traditionally been so distinct that the wall that divided them actually entered their cultural lexicon. The term "throw it over the wall" meant "send the code to the testers to see if they can break it." There was often animosity between the two sides, even if it was on a civil, professional level, because coders saw themselves as creators and they saw testers as people just there to destroy their creations. Testers, however, saw themselves as the guardians of quality assurance and product safety.

In those early days—we're talking the 1990s here—the turnaround time was also pretty slow. Sometimes buggy code would slip out and get into the marketplace, and software manufacturers would rely on the consuming public to report the problems back to them. The fixes would be included in the next upgrade. In those days, the feedback loop could take weeks or months.

This, of course, cannot happen today. Today's world counts time in milliseconds, not weeks. Google ranks pages (in part) according to their speed of download, and retailers know all too well the rate of shopping cart abandonment is also related to the speed of the website. Software applications, from word processing to ecommerce and cybersecurity, are so inextricably linked that delay is just not tolerated.

Some bugs still get through inevitably. But even if they didn't, the relentless innovations from the forces of cybercrime and hacking mean that continuous maintenance and fixes must occur, simply to keep pace with the realities of this industry. Improvements are still needed, and fixes must be swiftly deployed, which is why users regularly see upgrade notifications from the manufacturers of their phones, browsers, and operating systems. That's a continuous improvement mindset in action.

Other areas of software development have also been merging. Back in the day it was common to have a separate group that would be responsible for releasing the software to market. That is no longer the case. High performance demands more than that now. I build teams where the engineer who writes the code is also now the engineer who delivers that code to users. This is a completely open space—no walls. This allows agile teams to deploy code multiple times a day.

The engineer who writes the code is also the engineer who delivers that code to users.

Jez Humble points out that deployment frequency of this type demonstrates team maturity and efficiency (as I mentioned in Chapter 7). This is a key metric for measuring distributed software teams. In addition, my friend and colleague, Alex Martins, cowrote a great novelized account of the change process to continuous testing in the book *The Kitty Hawk Venture* (Apress, 2018).

So although the removal of these walls between coding and testing has become the new normal for software organizations, many less agile industries still operate in a much more old-school fashion. Many of these represent heavily regulated industries such as government, healthcare, and air and space technologies. But what this means is that, from a team management perspective, these organizations still hold a *traditional* mindset.

In competitive sailing, such as in regattas, it is common practice for a competing boat to position itself in such a way that it takes all the wind for itself, leaving its competitor in a kind of "wind shadow." Wind is linear, after all—it generally blows in a single direction. So the dominant boat can easily take the wind out of the sails of its competitor. This means that in a race, it's not always necessary for one boat to sail faster if, instead, it can make its competition sail slower. The same applies, obviously, to innovation and competition in the world of business and work.

With that in mind, the managers and senior executives of these "traditional mindset" organizations must come to terms with the reality that they must now embrace a continuous mindset in order to remain competitive and stay out of their opponents' shadows. The alternative is to stay frozen in time, which means someone else out there will evolve, innovate, and grab that wind for themselves.

The development and management of high-performance distributed teams is just one of these tangible examples of how a company can grab that wind for themselves by focusing on a new and much more timely approach to collaboration and productivity.

Breaking the A-to-Z Constraint with Smartboards

Here's one example of the continuous mindset that is beneficial both in its immediate application to creative thinking and by extension as a metaphor for an organization-wide change toward a distributed teams model.

In Chapter 12, I mentioned the use of the smartboard as a central focal point for online meetings as well as a tool of constructive synergy, and I also made mention of it in my discussion of memory in Chapter 13. Now I want to add to this the idea that the presence of creative thinking spaces like online smartboards will be another dividend of the distributed teams model and a further evolutionary step for productive workplaces.

In the brick-and-mortar workplace, walls exist in the form of cubicle dividers and as hour blocks on a calendar. These have always tended to segment people's minds, meaning that creative thinking could not flow organically or spontaneously. It had to wait until the next time people were back in a meeting or on a conference call, and sometimes this was too little, too late.

I will acknowledge that cubicles and offices helped in small part to provide some form of privacy for self-directed work, but I would suggest that unrealistic schedules and persistent distractions largely neutralized the capacity for cubicles to nurture the type of creative process that is vital for ongoing high performance.

In the human mind, creativity seldom appears in proper sequential order. Whether it's about writing a document or strategizing, the brain is an organic, electrochemical organ that functions holistically. It is not a serial information processor. It needs a tangible work surface to complete the activity.

The misguided need to create ideas sequentially was, for the most part, injected into people in grade school, following a set of teaching policies that were often decades out of date and remaining relevant to only the front end of a student population bell curve. That's why when I meet a student who has had academic problems in school, perhaps even to the point of dropping out or suffering some form of extreme anxiety or breakdown, I may say to them, "You didn't fail school—the system failed you."

The better approach to nurturing creativity is to flip the mandate around, moving it out of that A-to-Z sequence. With words, you have to get the ideas out first and edit them into proper order afterward. With teams, you have to place ideas and comments in a space where everyone can access and collaborate continuously and add or edit on their own time, either synchronously with others or asynchronously. That's what online smartboards and collaboration chat channels can do for high-performance distributed teams, removing the barriers that brick-and-mortar offices presented.

Throwing ideas up onto this smartboard surface and then taking time to review them gives teams opportunity to process the ideas anew, both individually and as a group, from wherever they happen to be and at whatever time suits them. This optimizes the use of short-term and long-term memory that I described in Chapter 13.

Building Continuous Knowledge Through the Wikipedia Model

At this point in time, most people have used or seen Wikipedia since online search tools inevitably serve it up in their search results. Wikipedia has yet to attain full credibility in some academic circles due to its lack of a verifiable peer review process that conforms to schools' existing traditions, but I would argue that it does actually have a form of peer review process, and it represents a new and continuous model of knowledge management ideally suited for high-performance teams.

Wikipedia is an online encyclopedia built on a collaborative website, using the Hawaiian word *wiki*, meaning "quick." Information about any topic is supplied by volunteers who possess subject matter expertise in a certain area.

Anyone can create or contribute to a Wikipedia entry, but when any addition or edit is made, it will be quickly pounced upon by those same subject matter experts who will be alerted to the existence of the new material and will move in to fact-check and demand citations and clarity. This helps maintain high standards of accuracy.

Though the occasional false posting or vandalism gets through temporarily, these are quickly found, challenged, corrected, or removed. What we as a global community receive is a knowledge base that evolves in real time—a continuous conscious record that can be accessed from anywhere.

The open source nature of Wikipedia represents to me that same type of open source, evolutionary mindset demonstrated by entrepreneurs like Elon Musk (whom I discussed in Chapter 5), with his company's groundbreaking approaches to space transport, electric cars, battery power, high-speed travel, and, before that, online commerce and banking.

Any organization can—and should—learn from and embrace the Wikipedia model, building their own internal knowledge base. Internal Wikis become an ever-evolving center of continuous knowledge, always on, and always accessible. They can be continuously updated and refined with new techniques, images, videos, augmented reality or virtual reality assistance, templates, and lessons and made available to team members as part of their own ongoing, continuous education while remaining proprietary to the individual organization.

This frees up employees to contribute and learn on their own time and also seek out solutions to immediate problems without needing to wait for a formalized chain of command—another example of empowerment at work.

Although you could argue that an internal Wiki could be equally accessible to a cubicle worker in an office, certainly it can, but the reality is that the culture of a brick-and-mortar workplace lends itself to a bias toward more traditional, static learning scenarios such as meetings, presentations, and documents in binders.

The Wiki model represents a quantum leap forward in continuous knowledge management and access and serves as a central pillar for progressive organizations of any type and especially those who are contemplating a distributed teams model.

Continuous Learning: Promoting Lifelong Learning Opportunities

Learning is a lifelong requirement. To get good at something, you have to practice it, do it, repeat it, and continue to learn and relearn. Even when you believe you have attained perfection, you will still only be perfect for that moment. Changing times and conditions mean that mastery must always be pursued; it can never truly be caught.

Learning, like smartboard-based creativity and Wiki-based knowledge, can also be continuous. In fact, these continuous learning strategies are already present in existing high-performance teams. The formalized approach to full-day classes is quickly being replaced by iterative online opportunities that can range from online classes through to snippets of knowledge captured on Twitter.

Microlearning Through Twitter

Twitter is much maligned for its ocean of offensive or irrelevant material propagated by people and bots alike, but the fact remains there are still a great many valuable thought leaders and experts who share their knowledge on that same platform, one tweet at a time. In my opinion, part of the definition of literacy for this new age is the ability to separate the wheat from the chaff—pulling the good information from a dense and ever-expanding field of material—and, equally importantly, knowing the importance of having to do just that, rather than waiting for someone else to deliver it for you. Microlearning through Twitter consists simply of identifying and following experts of high value and checking in once or twice per day to learn something new from them while ignoring all the unnecessary material.

Currently Twitter is the most commonly accessible medium with the greatest selection of experts to choose from. Other social media apps like Instagram and Reddit have their own value, but for the time being, Twitter still offers the best balance of accessibility and content.

Five or ten minutes a day of up-to-date microlearning through Twitter, just reading a curated collection of experts, is all that is needed.[1]

Hands-On Learning

As a leader, I want to ensure that the members of my distributed teams continue to learn and grow in their careers. But again, as a leader, I also want to ensure their learning goals are aligned with our collective voyage toward the North Star.

Suppose an employee wanted to learn a new programming language or technology. For this example, let's say we want an engineer to learn a new cutting-edge cloud development technology. Also, let's make the assumption the organization needs to move away from its traditional hosting infrastructure where its product is currently serving millions of users over the Internet. And to be clear, by traditional hosting I mean an infrastructure where the software requires servers running 24/7 at full capacity to serve its user base.

For some context in this example, in the world of cloud computing, a lack of elasticity or scalability is a problem. We now do business in an age where it is both possible and necessary to be able to scale servers up and down in a matter of seconds. In the world of online presence, customer demand for access to a company's website may require ten servers right now, but one hundred servers a minute later. Peaks in demand happen, but keeping a company's processing power at peak capacity at all times is a waste of money and energy. That's why highly elastic software solutions are needed—to ride the curve of demand, operate more efficiently, and respond to unprecedented scaling needs when they occur. I described an example of this in Chapter 7, when the company I worked for had to grow over 600 percent in a matter of a few hours during the early days of the pandemic due to an enormous increase in people needing to work and learn from home.

So, back to the team members' learning needs. The goal for leaders is to create an environment where team members learn about new industry technologies and then learn how to use them. But sending a team member to a full multiday course might not be the best course of action. Ninety-five percent of the time and money spent on this initiative would be wasted, as per the Ebbinghaus Forgetting Curve described in Chapter 13. In addition, the

---

[1]Check out www.linkedin.com/learning and www.udacity.com/

value that this person could have been delivering to customers is reduced to zero for the duration of the course.

High-performance team members love learning new technologies, and many have neither the patience nor the time for traditional learning. I prefer instead to identify individualized, compartmentalized learning opportunities that align team members with real-world situations where they can learn and then apply and improve their learning in relation to actual circumstances and business needs.

This could follow the pairing model in which a person with expertise invests the time to show a specific technique to another who then learns hands-on iteratively until they feel comfortable with the new skill or topic. Many people shy away from this teaching model because the domain expert feels it will take longer to show the other person than it would to perform the work themselves. This is true in that first instance, but as the person learns, there comes a point where knowledge is sufficiently transferred and the task can be handed over, freeing up the expert to focus on other valuable activities while also strengthening the relationship between both people. It also provides the learner an opportunity to grow, enhancing their desire to stay with the company and simultaneously providing the company with additional skilled resources and engaged team members. That's why pairing is an investment. It comes with tangible dividends.

In addition to pairing team members to learn from each other, this mindset of modular, on-demand education also supports the Wiki model, described earlier in this chapter, in which specific how-to's, including video examples, are made available to all team members and are continually updated.

This is always a triple win: team members stay happy because they are learning and applying their knowledge in the real world, users are happy because they receive better and faster user experiences, and the company is happy because it keeps moving toward its North Star.

Overall, the education still happens. But instead of being condensed inside a fixed number of hours, like a siloed room or the segments of Waterfall-based software development, it blends with the real-time flow of business and therefore aligns with the shift left, continuous testing model of DevOps and, equally importantly, the dynamic and responsive nature of work and innovation in this highly mobile era.

Career Ladder Learning

I mentioned the career ladder in Chapter 10 as an approach that can help distinguish between hiring someone for an existing job and hiring someone who aligns with the expectations and values for the job. In Chapter 12, I described how individual team members can and should use career ladders to design their own path toward their own personal North Star. I always like to emphasize the importance of people acknowledging their own aspirations and furthering their desire to keep moving forward in their careers. To use a boating metaphor, the career ladder is a chart that identifies all the possible routes and "markers" such as additional learning or skills development requirements that will help team members navigate their careers and achieve their own destinations.

The career ladder helps align job expectations with actual delivered performance. It is intended to put people on the same page, so it must be simple, objective, and constantly used as a reference. It should not only have the perspective from managers but also be used as a self-evaluation mechanism and the core of performance reviews. Leveraging the career ladder in this way allows managers to identify places where individual team members can identify opportunities to improve while best contributing to the overall business.

For example, if someone is not doing well on writing automated tests for their own code or requires a specific component of cybersecurity training, these can be identified as part of the ladder. The ladder is the guide; it gives a chance for the manager and employee to have a conversation and decide together what needs to be improved. It's a tool that helps individuals to align their company's expectations of them with continuous learning and vice versa. Whereas the image of a path is of a continuous journey, the ladder concept provides direction with clearly defined, iterative steps, ensuring education is never random, but instead offers yet another way for individuals to take proper steps toward their own North Star.

Education as a Service

Gone are the days when students had no choice but to trudge to a school building, laden down with heavy books and the anticipation of boring lectures and homework assignments to come. One of the most valuable developments of the 2010 decade was in discovering that education could be a distributed team activity and that a curriculum could be personalized not only by topic but also by source.

Traditional universities have been joined by startup schools who have made up for their lack of ivy league pedigree and physical buildings by offering timely, future-forward education delivered virtually. Many of these institutions also offer degree or certificate programs that blend courses from a variety of different schools and which are built around the needs and the schedules of each individual student.

In my opinion, people prefer to learn in real-life situations rather than classrooms. The best way to learn is through hands-on application. As such, traditional learning is shifting to education as a service because the world, like technology and innovation, is no longer being measured in years but in smaller units of time. As leaders of distributed teams, we need to be aware of that and be prepared to adapt and create environments that welcome and support continuous learning for employees with diverse skill sets and backgrounds in place of those traditional organizations that expect the perfect unicorn to knock on the front door asking for a job.

Flipped Learning

This is something that is close to my heart and represents the future of actual learning, in my opinion. It is something that the companies that I work with place high in priority.

There are two major features of the flipped learning model: first, it reverses the traditional ideas about classroom activities and homework. Rather than introduce new concepts as part of an in-class lecture, students are introduced to new material as homework, usually in the form of short videos or short articles. Then the online class time the following day is used for interaction, where students can ask questions and discuss the new information and fully tap into the instructor's experience.

This is how learning best happens and relates back to my hands-on learning approach that I described earlier in this chapter. When people can massage new information into their selves through experience and context, it becomes a tangible way of flattening the Ebbinghaus Forgetting curve and giving learning a more visible ROI.

Second, the flipped learning approach focuses on delivering differentiated, personalized learning experiences. This is the essence of the as-a-service economy in any industry—delivering customized, audience-of-one services, as and when they are needed, and, in the case of education, conforming to the learning style and life demands of the individual.

It may seem unconventional to those of us whose education and career path to date were forged in a more traditional linear process, but I believe this transition to continuous learning is just as much a next step in our social evolution. It's part of the *audience-of-one* approach, which is replacing the one-size-fits-all traditional approach. Flipped schooling is not just for school-age kids—it is also an excellent model for ongoing professional development and skills enhancement for members of a distributed team.

Just because these forms of education haven't happened before doesn't mean they can't happen now.

Key Takeaways

- The continuous mindset replaces the traditional linear, walled approach to progress. Industries like software development have formalized this, but it applies equally to other spheres of work.

- Smartboards represent an opportunity to open up the creative thinking space, especially among distributed teams.

- Knowledge gathering is a continuous process that can be maximized through microlearning and as-a-service-type education opportunities.

Learning from Mistakes

I was crewing in a regatta once where we failed big time. We failed, not because of any physical defect in the boat or its gear or even because of the weather. We didn't even fail because of the other teams' superior strength or talent, but because we made a mistake in not identifying and recovering properly from a team misalignment in communication.

At the start of the race, our captain shared the coordinates and final instructions with the crew, as is the practice, but these commands failed somehow to be fully understood by all the members of the team. Once we were underway, in a critical moment of the race, this inadequate communication meant we lost speed and momentum quickly. As a team, we had not been as aligned as we thought we were.

When you're sailing, you only have the wind as your power source, and how you guide the boat through the waters, reading the wind, the waves, and the currents, requires careful attention, skilled actions such as trimming of the sails, and a constant focus on weight distribution, including where all the members of the crew are positioned. This is where our misalignment converted into actual problems.

© Alberto S. Silveira Jr. 2021
A. S. Silveira Jr., *Building and Managing High-Performance Distributed Teams*,
https://doi.org/10.1007/978-1-4842-7055-4_15

We were going into a turn, gibing through a strong wind. As this situation unfolded, we, as a team, realized that we had not all heard the captain's commands correctly. Honestly, we should have fallen back on practiced procedures since it is vital to have a Plan B for times like these. But instead, we tried to improvise. We tried to rebalance the vessel in a turn using a new and spontaneous idea, one that had not been tested or agreed to by the team, and because of this, two of our crew went overboard. This is obviously one of the worst things that can happen to a vessel, on par with a collision or sinking.

The two were rescued by one of the many power boats that were on scene for just such a situation, given that this was a professional race, with safety crews everywhere. But the fact was we should have relied on those practiced procedures, but we didn't. We tried to wing it, and as a result we lost team communication, alignment, and cohesiveness and, for a little while, two of our crew.

As a necessary note to this story, in the interest of my One Team, One Heart philosophy, I must point out that the gender-specific term *man overboard* is still used in overboard situations, largely because of its distinct phonetics—the ah in man and the oh in overboard carry efficiently in noisy environments and across water and radio airwaves, much like the term *fire in the hole* does for announcing the intentional detonation of explosives. The term might be modernized and made gender neutral in time, but the protocol is to focus on safety and universal streamlined communication by using the male terminology for the time being. Frankly, I think the word *overboard!* by itself would work.

Mistakes Are Part of Continuous Progress

The reason I am sharing the *overboard* story is because, obviously, it wasn't one of my proudest moments as a crew member on a boat. But there are two lessons to take from this. The first is that mistakes are part of improvement, more specifically, part of continuous improvement; and, second, a mistake done by one should be shared by all.

I have already made mention of SpaceX in Chapters 4 and 10, but it makes sense to add another detail to the description of their process at this point, and that is to touch upon their very public *fail-forward* approach.

Elon Musk has a flair for publicity, something he shares with iconic figures like Thomas Edison, Albert Einstein, and Stephen Hawking. Not to take anything away from the genuine brilliance of these people, but Dr. Hawking is famous for telling prospective literary agents, when he was looking to publish his classic *A Brief History of Time*, that he wanted it to sell in airport bookstores. He broke away from the traditional, accepted model of the on-campus professorial scientist to spread his ideas to a wider audience.

Musk, too, in developing a new approach to rocketry that employed reusable parts, chose to buck the trend shared by companies in most industries, of burying their mistakes out of fear of media or shareholder retribution, and instead posted his mistakes on YouTube for everyone to see. This is a new way of thinking. It says, "Mistakes are part of progress and of improvement. Let's use them in a positive way."

I am not saying that Musk's approach is perfect. People have died in the pursuit of the SpaceX vision, and I respect their memory whenever I think of these approaches. Rocketry is extremely difficult and dangerous, and many people have given their lives throughout history in pursuit of space travel innovation, in every space agency in the world. But the idea of bringing mistakes out in the open goes far to reduce the prospects of those same mistakes happening again by opening up the narrative to an entire team of people who can see it on the same page at the same time and generate synergy.

Overall, going public with mistakes represents a newer form of thinking, perhaps brought on by the near-universal access to the Internet, which allows innovators like Musk to recognize there is far greater potential for progress to be gained by sharing their mistakes with a global community of minds than there is in hiding them and risking repetition of those same mistakes and much slower progress.

When a mistake or serious issue occurs, it is vital that every person on the team learns something about it. The day a team stops learning together, it will remain vulnerable, and those same mistakes will occur again. When mistakes happen and no learning and no closure follow, this can also impact morale, which can promote a culture of blame and will inevitably slow progress.

A distributed team that works together and that embraces the *One Team, One Heart* concept will be well suited for holding dynamic meetings in which conversation and brainstorming serve to proactively manage mistakes and work on solutions. There is great truth in the concept of the whole being greater than the sum of its parts, and this is eminently true when working on problem solving and creative thinking. Such actions could also succeed in the traditional on-premises workspace; in fact, they have, but the standard obstacles of getting many people in a room together at the same time make it less optimum than that which can be achieved through a distributed teams model.

In a successful distributed team, the whole is always greater than the sum of its parts.

Mistakes Usually Have Deeper Roots

For decades, when companies sought to discover where a problem came from, they would look for its root cause. Though this is better than not doing anything at all, the problem with this technique is that there is a tendency, once the root cause has been discovered, to view it in isolation.

Isolation and centrality are hallmarks of the hierarchical command-and-control culture that dominated commerce and industry in the decades leading up to the present. But as we have seen, the structure behind the distributed team is a holistic one in which the group functions as an organism that does not need a center. That same holistic concept can apply to problem solving and problem management.

We are seeing this now in medicine, where more and more medical practitioners and researchers are breaking away from the rigid approach of finding a singular root cause for a singular malady and are instead taking a broader, more holistic approach that factors in a much wider range of influences. In addition, the medical field is a shining example of the power of distributed teams, with innovations and discoveries being made daily, in many cases by people whose age or physical location would have barred them from participation in an earlier era.

The holistic approach to problem solving is why I prefer the term contributing factors over root cause. As I described in Chapter 12, choice of words matters. It makes a real difference in eliciting the right outcomes through comprehensible messaging.

Giving "Five-Why" the Continuous Edge

When there is a problem within an organization, system, or team, it makes sense to get to what seems to be the singular origin of that problem. If your boat seems to be sinking slowly, you can spend valuable time bailing the water out of the boat or you can go down below decks to identify the source of the leak. I have no disagreement with this concept of searching for the leak, but it's where people stop searching that I see opportunity for improvement.

One of the easiest traditional root cause analysis techniques has always been the five-why procedure (Figure 15-1), in which you ask "why?" to every statement that describes a problem, ostensibly drilling down to its root. A five-why root cause analysis of our situation that caused two crew members to fall overboard might have gone something like this:

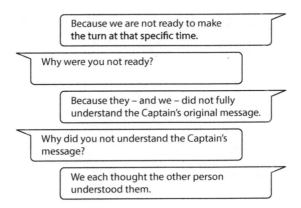

Figure 15-1. Five why's

This brief discussion identifies the root cause of my team's accident. This accident did not belong only to the two crew members who fell overboard; it belonged to all of us. In addition, because we decided to not fall back to Plan B, but instead chose to improvise a move we had not practiced before under those circumstances, things got worse.

But this five-why discussion, although correct in its execution, does not capture everything. There's more to this situation. There are more questions that can be asked and more contributing factors to be identified. There is a continuous mindset that can be applied here, by pursuing something more than a single, simple root cause. A series of ongoing five-why analyses should follow on from this discussion, starting with any or all of these:

- Why did the captain's message have different interpretations in the first place?

- Why didn't the team repeat its understanding back to the captain as a group?

- Why hadn't the team anticipated and discussed the unexpected scenarios?

- Why wasn't Plan B followed?

- Why were the crew not adequately drilled in the correct procedure?"

When you have more than one five-why questioning system, they get connected in a shape that looks a lot like the bones of a fish, and this is appropriately called a fish bone analysis (Figure 15-2).

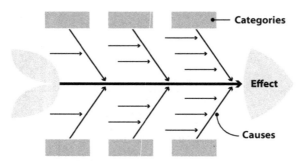

Figure 15-2. Fish bone analysis

Each five-why analysis becomes one of these bones of the fish, and each of these bones becomes a contributing factor to a larger solution.

Traditional root cause analysis can be effective in identifying the apparent source of a problem, but people tend to stop once they hit that first "aha" moment, and they don't go further to examine the broader context that gave rise to the problem. They stick with a bone and they don't go for the whole fish. There is seldom just one single root cause: there's always a combination of events that cause the issue, and that's why I prefer to call them contributing factors.

Once this is accepted as an ongoing process, an organization empowers itself with the ability to flip an old method of finding cause into an ongoing model of team-based continuous improvement.

A Mistake Done by One Should Be Shared by All

The next part of this concept ties the open source approach to acknowledging mistakes, highlighted by the SpaceX example previously discussed, to the open community of the distributed team. It can be surprising just how much wisdom can be uncovered when team members are given the opportunity to speak in open, distributed forums.

In this way, mistakes truly become opportunities for continuous improvement, and they also help drive team engagement and solidarity through a mutual problem solving experience.

The InnoCentive Model

When Colgate-Palmolive wanted to find a better way of getting toothpaste into tubes during the packaging process, they turned to their internal research and development department—but as great as these engineers and designers were, they could not solve the problem. So with the traditional, hierarchical brick-and-mortar approach not workable, the company decided to crowdsource a solution. They posted their problem at InnoCentive.com, a website that brings external experts into the fold, soliciting innovative ideas and providing financial incentives for doing so.

Colgate-Palmolive's challenge was answered by an electrical engineer who immediately knew that putting a positive electrical charge on the fluoride within the toothpaste while grounding the plastic tube would attract toothpaste to the tube, essentially pulling it into place.[1]

This is just one of many success stories that organizations like InnoCentive deliver, basically by combining the concepts of crowdsourcing, distributed teams, and open source idea sharing to solve problems that could not be solved internally.

In the software development business, many companies employ a similar, open source approach to testing once their products have reached the market, hiring experts to search for defects in the software. This is called a bug bounty program.

To me this reveals the enormous potential that a distributed team, including third-party partners, offers to an organization's future, whether the topic for discussion is a mistake that has been made, a challenge that exists, or an opportunity for innovation. When these are shared, rather than compartmentalized, the potential for success increases exponentially.

A Big Mistake/Learning Opportunity: The Twitter Hack

In July 2020, the Twitter accounts belonging to some of the world's most recognizable people, including Barack Obama and Joe Biden, as well as corporate sites including Uber and Apple, tweeted out the same message—an obscure Bitcoin sale offering. Few people were fooled by the message, which was obviously a scam, although enough people responded to allegedly allow the perpetrators to rake in over $100,000 in Bitcoin.[2]

The most worrying aspect of this hack was how the scammers managed to infiltrate the "blue check mark" accounts of numerous high-profile people and companies. Given the pivotal and hugely influential role that Twitter has made on the world stage, its security and invulnerability were considered beyond essential.

---

[1]Retrieved from InnoCentive.com. www.ideaconnection.com/open-innovation-success/Method-to-Get-Fluoride-Powder-into-Toothpaste-Tubes-00057.html
[2]Iyengar, Rishi. (July 15, 2020). "Twitter accounts of Joe Biden, Barack Obama, Elon Musk, Bill Gates, and others apparently hacked". CNN Business. www.cnn.com/2020/07/15/tech/twitter-hack-elon-musk-bill-gates/index.html. Retrieved July 15, 2020.

The hack happened through social engineering, a technique in which bad actors connect with people—not the computers or the networks, but people—by impersonating suppliers or managers, sending fake emails or phone calls from spoofed addresses, and basically worming their way into a system by creating a relationship of confidence or influence with people on the inside.

It's the cyber equivalent of an office that is protected with magnetic doors that need pass-cards to open, but whose employees are nice enough to allow strangers in without challenge. Why should a thief bother trying to knock down the door or hack the security system when it is easier to stand in the lobby and pretend to search for the pass-card in their briefcase or pockets? Inevitably a good-natured, unwitting employee will let them in.

This happens all too often, because people are nice, they are generally trusting of others, and they are also too busy to think critically about every situation that confronts them, and that's the problem.

As I have stated a couple of times already, a big part of the future of work lies in soft skills. These are skills like empathy that allow for trust and collaboration to happen within teams, but they are also skills like critical thinking, which could and should stop someone from getting fooled by social engineering hacks.

Although there have been many other hacks, breaches, and incidents and some much larger, like SolarWinds, in my opinion, this particular Twitter hack story should have been Agenda Item Number 1 at Monday morning huddles in every company, everywhere, no matter what department they work in. It's an example of addressing a perpetually evolving, continuous challenge of security that has, at its core, a human element. As such it should be matched with a perpetually evolving, continuous process of human learning and awareness skills.

The fact that this Twitter hack story wasn't Agenda Item Number 1 reminds me of the types of online security training that big enterprises force employees to take. In general, the courses are sterile, out of date, and certainly not engaging. That's where the cracks appear in the process and where failure and thieves sneak in. It's also an example of where continuous improvement really comes into play. Companies should focus on and invest in building a culture of security that is continuous and evolving.

After all, the bad guys are already doing this. You can think of hackers and cybercriminals as a business unto themselves. They never stop reinventing their expertise. These are people who are constantly, continuously seeking innovation in the cybercrime industry. They pivot, communicate, and capitalize on the talents and passions of their own distributed teams in real time. They are riding the Deming Cycle. They have already left the set-and-forget world.

It might seem unusual to glorify the bad guys in this way, but learning is about observation as much as it is about action. Black hat hackers may operate outside the law, but they are still a business and in most cases are well organized. They serve as an unlikely role model for the rest of us.

Avoiding Mistakes by Slowing to Optimum Operational Speed

Technology never works alone, either as the hero or the culprit in business processes. It is the interaction between people and their tools that will either generate innovation, progress, and success or will doom an organization to mediocrity and failure. It has thus far allowed us to do many more things more quickly, but that hasn't always resulted in a proportional increase in productivity or profitability. It now offers us the opportunity to do these things from many more places, without need for a center. And so the luxury of speed must be carefully considered because as the old adage so clearly states, "more haste, less speed."

There is a pattern of signal processing that goes on in the brain that has been perfected over hundreds of thousands of years. The mind needs to process what it takes in, and much of this requires a careful balance between instinct-based reflexes and the more cerebral actions of thinking things through.

We are at a point in human evolutionary history where we can't actually keep up with the speed of our own information. This is most easily demonstrated by the compulsion most people feel to read and respond to email and messages immediately, regardless of the situation. Even driving a car—piloting two tons of steel and flammable gasoline down the road at 80 feet per second—is not enough to stop people from responding to their text messages. This has little to do with the words in the sent message and much more to do with the fact that the human nervous system perceives the message as an urgency and reacts to it without thinking.

This leads to two more concepts that help put high performance into distributed teams.

Taking the Time to Read, Think, and Write

People who work according to the distributed teams model enjoy a significant time advantage. Just the lack of a regular commute is a major benefit. A one-hour commute done twice daily (to the office and home again), 48 weeks a year, equals 480 hours, which equals 20 full twenty-four-hour days or, more fittingly, 60 eight-hour workdays. That's two work months per year won back, simply by not commuting to a different building to do it.

My goal, with my teams, is not to fill this won-back time with even more low-level priorities, but to encourage quality of thought, quality of communication, and quality of community.

In the traditional brick-and-mortar workplace, the sending of emails was done as a supposed improvement over time-consuming meetings and delays, but as everyone knows, it merely resulted in mountains of emails—ergonomic inflation, a variation of Brooks's Law described in Chapter 6. The contributing factors of this problem involved more than a messaging system: the culture of the in-person workplace created the monster of email because no one was willing to identify a more holistic method of getting people together to collaborate, except, ironically, at off-site team-building events.

As such, the essence of high performance for distributed teams is not overt haste, but speed gained through more effective communications and thought processing techniques, of which the smartboard emerges as a prime example.

Writing on a smartboard is an ideal creative thinking tool because writing by hand is organic. The thinking brain synchronizes better with the pace and the motion of handwriting than of typing on a keyboard or texting on a phone. It's a haptic relationship, meaning the sense of touch is directly involved. Of course, the world has come to rely on the connected computer for pretty much everything we do, and I am not here to seek its removal. However, for those crucial times when clear, creative thought is required from my team members, individually as well as in group online meetings, I am going to ask that some of that time saved in commuting be invested in working a little slower, so that the hand and mind work in unison with those of other team members. In the end this will result in better work, done more quickly. It's a paradox that seems to strike directly against the go-fast modern work ethic, but yields better output.

Taking the Time to Lead

When it comes to managing teams, many managers are insecure or uncertain about their own leadership skills, and with good reason. Even a great leader needs time to think things through, take in all the facts, balance opposing viewpoints, and basically work things out before coming to a decision. This cannot be done when the leader's mind is constantly overrun by those same external stimuli such as email, most of which are low priority, disguised as high priority.

This lack of leadership confidence is not necessarily because leaders lack the skills to manage, but because they lack the time and space to use those skills to their fullest. When it comes to managing teams, whether they are distributed or onsite, the fundamental principles of leadership demand what they have always demanded: time, depth, and attention. These things must be applied at that moment when a leader speaks to a team or to an employee, but they must also be applied before that, during those moments of planning and reflection. These are moments invested that help shape ideas and thoughts.

Leadership requires a depth that follows its own triangular structure: the before, during, and after. A leader must prepare to lead by taking time to understand the people and the situations involved. Leadership requires in-the-moment skills as I have described in Chapter 4 and also requires analysis after the fact, at that moment when a leader looks back upon what was said, how it was received by the team, and what was learned.

The pace of the modern workplace has stripped away the time, energy, and self-permission required for these "before" and "after" segments, and this, in turn, has often diluted the effectiveness of the "during" segment.

This concept of taking the time to think clearly becomes another lesson that I can take from my "overboard!" story at the beginning of this chapter. In business, innovation and continuous improvement are vital, yes, but deployment of change should never be done on spec. It's not wise to change a process while the race is on.

If you are in an emergency situation, for example, your mission-critical systems have gone down, you must follow your procedures and standards. If your building is literally on fire, now would not be the time to try to discuss improvements to the emergency exits. You must follow the procedures as they are. You must follow the people who have been trained in emergency evacuation or IT security or sailing a boat, as the case may be. There will be time for review later.

This kind of wisdom might sound like common sense, but in my experience, common sense—that is to say, sensible shared philosophy—is in perpetual short supply. And even when it has been established, it tends to evaporate over time.

My observation is that what happens naturally, especially in urgent situations, is that humans have a tendency to adapt to what is happening. This is natural. It is part of the fight-or-flight reflex that prioritizes instinct and adrenaline over careful process. Some might argue that if this is the natural course of things—that reaction is superior to reason—this must be the right way to go. But in thinking like that, one must also consider that nature never concerned itself with the safety of the individual. Nature thinks in terms of millions of creatures and millions of years. So the fight-or-flight reflex may benefit the evolution of a species over time, but little thought or compassion will be given to you and your team as individuals in the moment.

The Time Hunter-Gatherer

When agriculture was established 12,000 years ago, humans freed themselves from the burden of having to expend calories to collect calories. Before this, hunter-gatherers had to work hard to find food. This was a vicious circle. Those who expended more energy than the food could replace tended to die in great numbers.

Agriculture allowed civilizations to grow and store more calories than a group of people needed to simply exist day to day. This allowed for the development of crafts, towns, and economies, since not everyone had to hunt or even farm. Languages and writing then allowed for the storage and processing of thought. Every major innovation since has helped create a better way for humans to stave off death and actually thrive.

The digital era that started in the late twentieth century has crossed us backward over an evolutionary equator, into a phase where we can no longer keep up with the data that our devices are feeding us. Collectively, our capacity to think through the information has been overtaken by its sheer volume. Critical thinking has been replaced by social media in which every person can find a source of news that matches their existing biases and beliefs. We have once again become a type of hunter-gatherer in which the effort of managing information flow exceeds our capacity to handle it, thus reducing us to working at a deficit, just like our preagricultural ancestors.

I feel that by moving away from the brick-and-mortar workplace, the hive of centralized activity, and replacing it with a dynamic and distributed form of work that matches the needs of the individual alongside those of the organization represents a supreme example of human evolution moving ahead once again, most significantly by allowing us to reconnect with our collective natural thought process and reap its genius in every area of life.

Key Takeaways

- Mistakes are part of the continuous learning process, and their value should be recognized.

- Mistakes should also be open sourced and shared rather than hidden, since they provide opportunity for learning and innovation.

- The greatest dividend of the distributed teams model will be time—time that can be reinvested into higher-quality thought and action.

Setting Sail: Outfitting for Distributed Teams

As we have seen throughout this book, when you work as a crew member on a boat, the working conditions must be optimized. Cleanliness and order are vital. Every piece of equipment must be clean, stored, and ready. This is what the term *shipshape* means, by the way. If you have ever used that term to describe an office or a project that is in good order, you are using a nautical term that has been used for centuries, to describe a vessel that is ready to go to sea.

A vessel that is dirty or that has oil on the deck or whose lines (ropes) are showing signs of wear or whose safety equipment is out of date or improperly stowed is inviting injury or worse. A boat needs the right equipment, set up the right way, in order for crews to move it successfully forward.

© Alberto S. Silveira Jr. 2021
A. S. Silveira Jr., *Building and Managing High-Performance Distributed Teams*,
https://doi.org/10.1007/978-1-4842-7055-4_16

The same applies to a well-structured distributed team. During the pandemic lockdowns, many people who were forced to work from home for perhaps the first time found themselves doing their work in less than optimum conditions. Some were working in the living room, struggling to concentrate while the kids played or wrestled with their own schoolwork or watched TV close by. This type of arrangement generates tension and frustration, which is counterproductive to work and bad for family relationships.

Many people currently don't have the ideal physical space at home, and very few fully understand the security requirements of their home network, computer, and applications, which represents a significant weak link in any organization's infrastructure.

Distributed teams need legitimate work conditions and training to be able to deliver their work correctly. As I have described, legitimate work conditions include technology, culture, and a renewed approach to time management and leadership. That is what it means to be shipshape.

Distributed teams need legit work conditions and education to be shipshape.

Attaining synergy is not always easy, but nor is it impossible. Leaders who seek to establish a successful distributed teams culture need to think about providing those adequate workspaces, hardware, tools, connectivity, logistics, and ergonomics to their teams, to match the evolution of the culture. This will make all the difference between "being at home trying to work" and "working from home."

The new normal following the pandemic lockdown period will be an opportunity for companies to use what they have learned about the very real benefits that the distributed teams model offers. As I hope I have shown, it is not just about producing pieces of work from a physically separate location; it speaks to a far more enhanced dynamic, involving hiring and care of individual team members, leveraging their skills and enthusiasm, and crafting a company's voyage based on the chemistry that great people share and a leadership vision that recognizes it. It's a new model for some, but it is one that would have happened even if there had been no pandemic. There were already the beginnings of a gradual shift toward a more empowered workforce, through the development of the audience-of-one model that spans the B2C and B2B worlds equally.

Distributed Does Not Mean Disconnected

Just because the model of a distributed team is based on people working from wherever they are does not mean they should never get together. In the companies I have worked with or consulted to, I have made it a point to ensure the team gets together in person at least once per year. This is not only for work but it's also for fun. It's for the type of bonding and interaction that can only happen in a casual and playful environment.

Being in distributed teams doesn't mean there must be no face-to-face in-person interaction. Being distributed is about trust, and an in-person connection plays an important role in developing trust. The same thing applies for on-premises teams as well, of course. Even if they work on the same floor, people seldom get the opportunity to connect, yet it's vital that they do.

Being distributed is about trust, and an in-person connection plays an important role in developing trust.

There is great joy in connection. Many times in my life I have been fortunate to observe this joy, where two people, who have only known each other from an email address or as a voice on the phone or maybe as an avatar or a face on a video chat, get to hug, get to talk about each other's families, and just expand their social circle and the depths of their own life experiences.

As a result, this connection helps to build the synergy for creative minds to share ideas, brainstorm, and come up with actions that will solve challenges or end up in new innovation.

Physical Setup

It is often assumed that distributed employees will be able to get more done day to day simply due to the elimination of their commute. But as I just mentioned, there is a big difference between *being at home trying to work* and *working from home*. What sort of space should distributed team members have in order to do their work most efficiently? This is something that often goes overlooked by managers who are dealing with people working from different geographic locations for maybe the first time. They suppose that the employee's own home-based setup will suffice by default. But this is often not the case.

A place of work needs the right setup to do the job, with up-to-date hardware and software and a secure and reliable Internet connection. Team members ideally need a dedicated space, with an ergonomically comfortable chair, desk, and lighting, just as they would have in a traditional office. For many, this means using a dedicated room or corner of a room, rather than working from the kitchen or living room table.

The workspace should be a zone of focus and not distraction. If there are other family members present and there's no opportunity to close oneself off completely, it can still be done with sound barriers, like sound-suppressing headphones playing music or pink noise as a barrier. There are a great many channels on places like Spotify that provide *music for study* or *music for concentration* that make it much easier for people to work, even when the family TV is on in the same room.

For video chats, there will need to be some form of sound insulation. It's easy enough to mute yourself when you are not talking, but when it comes time to speak up, the microphone will pick up background sound.

In addition, a work schedule itself might need to be built around homelife responsibilities, such as walking the dog or picking the kids up from school. This is a new element in the workday, but it need not be a problem. It is easy to let team members know when you will be available, just through clear time management and communication habits. This is a great opportunity to use the overcommunication techniques mentioned in Chapter 13, by updating status messages and online calendars to show availability and non-availability. It is also a great example of managing expectations, since the other team members will know when to expect a reconnection and can reorganize their day accordingly.

This is exactly what work-life integration is all about, and it is at the heart of the distributed teams concept. The net result is a gain for an organization, since team members can capitalize on a more balanced existence to deliver the required output on time. It's different than working in the office, but that's kind of the point. It's different and I think it's better.

Security is another key aspect that often doesn't get the required attention. One of the most vulnerable spaces in a home office is usually the network, which is seldom secured and might still have the Internet router, for instance, operating under its default password. The router should be secured and every device in the household that connects to it, including non-work-related devices like kids' school computers, and Internet of Things appliances (smart doorbells, Wi-Fi-connected smoke/CO_2 alarms) should be secured as well.

In the distributed teams I've built, I like to establish guidelines that require team members to encrypt their computer hard disk as well as to enable 2FA (two-factor authentication) on their company IdP (Identity Provider) accounts. Simple security measurements like this can reduce risks to the users, the employees, and to the organization.

At first glance, all of these items appear to be very costly—additional entries on a department's quarterly operating costs ledger. But in general, the costs of setting up a distributed teams workplace, including the purchase of new gear, are far lower than the costs of hosting these same people on the floor space of a building. In fact, even prior to the pandemic lockdown, companies were already eyeing the significant cost savings they could enjoy by removing floor space—meeting rooms, cubicle areas, dining areas—literally shrinking their footprint as their employees went virtual.

Creating the Connected Culture

The culture of any successful team anywhere starts and ends with people. People need to feel part of something, and they need to feel respected. They need to know they can reach you when they need you, but also that you will leave them to do their work. They need a balance of Focus Time, Collaboration Time, and Catch-up Time. In addition, they also need informal socialization time. They look to leaders to lead by example and to trust them to deliver their work, rather than micromanage them.

Workplace culture starts with vision and thrives on continuous feedback. It requires some central communication points—hangouts, breakout rooms, clear spaces to share information or have conversations. It helps to have a centralized knowledge base filled with definitions, how-to guides, standards, and everything else a team member might want to know about while setting out to complete the work.

It is key to have **one single source of truth** for everything instead of having many versions or bits and pieces all over the place that could cause confusion. Information must be easily accessible and searchable by everyone. That helps human communication. That helps connect people. And that is a key component for high-performance teams. It is the lack of this single source of truth that becomes the source of many of the pitfalls that teams encounter, whether they are on-premises or distributed.

> *Environment influences behavior, collective behavior creates culture, and culture drives results.*
>
> —Kristi Woolsey, *Designing Culture* (2016)

Tribal Togetherness

People are instinctively tribal. For hundreds of thousands of years, we have arranged ourselves into groups or tribes under a leader. We identify ourselves through symbols, colors, and brands. We have the need to connect with others and form groups; it is part of human nature. This is no different for distributed teams. Team members still need to feel connected, with you, their leader, as well as with each other. It's not just about the work. It can't just be about the work, and the work itself won't happen without adequate team building. That's why I always bring my distributed team members together whenever I can, virtually or in-person.

Think about the activities that might appeal to the members of your distributed teams that can promote this environment of togetherness:

- "TED Talks"-type series department-wide in which guest speakers address and engage with the audience. For instance, I promote to my teams what I call Show & Tell. This typically happens once a month for one hour during lunch where any team member is encouraged to sign up. Each session has three presentations of 15 minutes each.

- Open source projects and active blog posts that can help expose great work to the community and increase recognition and the sense of belonging.

- Hackathon events where team members have the opportunity to work with other team members from other teams in creative and innovative solutions.

- Feedback mechanisms where people, individually or as a group, are encouraged to share thoughts that could lead to improvements, without having to wait for the traditional review cycles.

- *Unconference*-type events where the participants drive the topics and the execution of the events. That creates an outlet for people to connect on the topics they are passionate about.

- Self-organized events where teams can create and purchase T-shirts, stickers, winter gloves, or similar types of custom team branding merchandise.

The idea behind these types of events and items is to generate a sense of community outside of the day-to-day activity of work. I have participated in and facilitated a fair amount of corporate meetings, and it is absolutely rewarding when you see team members connecting to each other naturally, in an organic way. The human connection created in these kinds of events goes a long way to maximize everyone's investment in the team.

Online Work Is Different

During the year 2020, companies were more or less forced to adopt the distributed teams model even if they had not planned to. With employees in mandatory lockdown, there was no other choice. Their employees were at home, connected only by their Internet technologies. Many companies had projects they had to deliver, along with meetings and all the other parts of the workday, which now had to be done through video chats.

When it came to events such as presentations and training sessions, it soon became apparent that a full day spent in front of a screen, watching a presenter present, is more fatiguing than watching that same presenter speak in person. This has to do in part with eye fatigue. In a meeting room or office, people are free to let their eyes move around the room, varying their length of focus, from the presenter to the board, to a colleague, to the clock on the wall, and to everything else.

On a video chat, by contrast, everything happens on a screen, and your key point of contact is the camera lens, which protocol suggests you focus on in order to make it look like you are looking directly at the other people in the meeting. Although you are technically free to look around your own workspace or turn off your camera, that is not seen as ideal since it looks like you are disinterested.

Being forced to stare at a fixed focal length for many hours is tiring for the eyes and brings on fatigue much more quickly. I like to use the 50-minute rule instead of one hour for meetings. Or 25 minutes instead of 30. The rule of thumb is to not fill people's calendars with nonstop back-to-back meetings during the whole day. People need to have meals, bio breaks, and stretch a little bit in order to be able to provide their best.

Between the fatigue factor and the need for Focus Time, Catch-up Time, and Collaboration Time, a day can quickly fill up for the members of your distributed team. And that is something that distributed teams have in common with on-premises teams. There seems to never be enough hours in the day.

But I would venture to rephrase this last comment. It's not that there are not enough hours in the day. It's that there is not enough time management in the day. For decades, companies have been drifting into wasteful habits in the workplace. Meetings that run on too long, unnecessary status checks, detailed estimation conversations about far future projects, uncountable emails—the list goes on. Life in the office has more ways to waste time than to save it, which is why time management courses and leadership books sell so well: everyone is looking for the secret on how to do it better, but the culture is one that has grown passively and has created most of its own faults.

The new generation of professionals seeking a more flexible work-life balance approach and fully aware of the potential of distributed technology offers a new conscious slant toward the high-performance workplace, one that puts *management* back into time management and *performance* into a high-performance team.

What is required is a conscious awareness of the potential of every individual person. Some are morning people; some are night owls. Some are Type A; some are Type B. The trick to devising a structure for high-performance distributed teams is to not assume there is just one. There is not a "one-size-fits-all model." This demands more of a personalized approach that encourages the best from a diverse group of people. It is critical that team members share their preferences and get aligned on what is best for them individually and collectively as a team.

The key goal is to get people to step off their metaphorical hamster wheel and realize that more can be done by proactively planning time than can be achieved by reactively juggling tasks. One of the best methods for this is the Pareto Principle, otherwise known as the 80/20 rule.

The 80/20 Rule

Here is a summary of the Pareto Principle, as described in *Cool Time: A Hands-On Plan for Managing Work and Balancing Time* (Wiley, 2005), written by Steve Prentice:

> The 80/20 Rule is also known as the Pareto Principle, and is one of the most important concepts of all of business life because it applies as a useful and relevant model to understand both how things are and how they should be.
>
> In 1906, the Italian economist Vilfredo Pareto observed that twenty percent of the Italian people owned eighty percent of his country's accumulated wealth. It was the official start of a famous tool of illustration now known as the Pareto Principle, or the 80/20 rule. It is a versatile principle that helps describe the many areas of human activity in which a small amount of something has significant impact over a larger amount.
>
> The actual proportions, eighty and twenty, are not as important as their symbolism. It does not have to be exactly eighty percent, for example, but it illustrates some very dynamic points such as "eighty percent of the value of a meeting happens during twenty percent of its actual duration."
>
> There are dozens of these examples in all areas of life, but the one that makes the most sense in terms of time management is the following:
>
> You get more done when you invest 20 percent of your time to manage the other 80 percent.

How can this be? Because planning and doing gets more done than just doing alone. People who simply take on tasks without allowing time to plan them out or delegate or negotiate find themselves on a hamster wheel, perpetually working but never catching up.

One of the greatest techniques of effective time management is to ensure that the right tasks are done the right way, and this requires investing time not only for planning but also for building a kind of credit rating with co-workers through collaborative conversation, intelligent delegation, learning how not to procrastinate, and even allowing time to eat properly, both breakfast and lunch as well as snacks in between. All of this has an impact on them as well as you. At the moment, what is most important to recognize is the concept that more can be done by carving 20 percent out of the 100 percent and using it strategically.

What should be applied in this 20 percent of a person's time? How about managing expectations? Sending out calls or messages to stakeholders or clients letting them know when you're available to meet or when you will be able to return messages in detail. This gives them the satisfaction of knowing they will be cared for and frees you up from having to address people's requests when you are in the middle of managing something else. The 20 percent can also be used to plan and prioritize your day more efficiently, factoring in time for other necessities—work related and home related—and also prioritizing your highest-value tasks for the time of day when you are at your physical and mental best.

Another use of the 20 percent is in networking and relationship management. A person who is too busy to take time to talk to other team members loses an immediate opportunity to build trust and generate support from colleagues and managers.

On our boats, we spend time before preparing for and discussing the trip, checking all the gear and the weather twice, and filing a float plan. All of this is time spent not sailing—it's part of that 20 percent—but because of this investment, the bulk of the time can be given over to the act and enjoyment of boating.

For distributed teams, the relevance of the 80/20 rule speaks to the reality that time management has always been important. In the brick-and-mortar workplace, it helped people prioritize tasks in the face of constant interruptions, meetings, and email. Although some might think those things don't happen for distributed team members, they do. As such it is vital for people working in the distributed teams model to learn how to structure their days along the 80/20 model, for the same reasons. The interruptions, meetings, and messages will still occur, regardless of where a person works. In fact, to quote Anne Chow, CEO of AT&T, "Work is no longer a place."[1]

---

[1] www.linkedin.com/pulse/att-ceo-anne-chow-keynotes-economist-event-series-new-demotte-kramer/

Seeking Purpose

Why would I want to teach someone a skill that they might want to take and use somewhere else? Because that's *purpose*. Purpose is the desire to do something that has meaning, that's bigger than yourself. Purpose is about autonomy. It's what people of all ages seek as they carve their own path through life.

Giving people the freedom to work their own way and to learn their own way is a method for rewarding them with autonomy, and usually, rather than fly away, they will stay, comfortably aware of their own place within the distributed teams structure.

I started this book by describing my love for boating, and I have used examples from my boating and sailing lives as allegories throughout. I wish to conclude by just adding a bit more about how I learned how to sail and how, in doing, I found purpose.

I started learning to sail in a lagoon near my hometown of Florianópolis, Brazil. We were a team of three: myself, a friend—whom I have continued to sail with to this very day—and our instructor. This was a small team formation in a very controlled environment, in safe conditions, where we were able to learn the basics and some of the finer points of sailing, no matter which direction the wind was coming from, even when it blew from the front. These exercises allowed me to build my confidence, even though—or especially because—we managed to flip the boat a couple of times.

I was able to take the lessons that I learned in that lagoon to help me find my purpose and to channel it. My new skills as a sailor helped me manage boats out on the open ocean. At the same time, I converted those same lessons into techniques for managing soccer teams around my town, and this eventually led to me leaving my small hometown in Brazil, crossing the Equator, and starting to work in, and then oversee, high-tech teams in organizations in the Big Apple, United States.

Was there fear in any of these situations? Sure there was. Fear is natural. It's the body's way of saying, "Are you sure you want to do this?" Feeling fear is not something to be ashamed of. It's how you handle the fear that counts, and I believe that going out there, whether it's the open ocean or the world of business, with a strong team around you and with a clear sense of purpose, you can neutralize the fear, and you can achieve your goals, even if it takes more than one try to do so.

I still shake my head sometimes, when I see these really smart people who now report to me. Some are American; others have come from other parts of the world, just like me. And these brilliant people are reporting to me? That's when I realize, "Yeah, I really learned how to sail, and yeah, I really found my purpose."

And that's why I decided to write this book. I think every person has the right to experience the exhilaration that I felt and still feel every time I take my own boat out past the safety of the harbor's breakwater and its lighthouse, out onto the open water. People who wish to lead need to understand the people who work in teams. People who wish to pursue their professional passions also need to understand the dynamics of teams and of all the people and tasks that hold them together.

Teams no longer need a single physical place to define them. They no longer need a room to contain them. In the decade to come, more and more people will recognize that in fact the opposite is true, that the greatest teams exist when there is no single place at the center, but instead that true togetherness and progress happen when the team members hold themselves together and support themselves through the tangible strength of a distributed model.

The future lies forward for those who want to build it together.

Key Takeaways

- Distributed teams need appropriate physical tools and settings, just like they would in an office.

- A connected culture needs a single source of truth along with awareness of people's tribal instincts.

- Giving people the freedom to find their own purpose is the best way of keeping a distributed team together.

Index

© Alberto S. Silveira Jr. 2021

A. S. Silveira Jr., *Building and Managing High-Performance Distributed Teams*, https://doi.org/10.1007/978-1-4842-7055-4

CPSIA information can be obtained
at www.ICGtesting.com
Printed in the USA
LVHW080749170521
687632LV00004B/162